1,000
FACTS ABOUT
SHARKS

BY SARAH WASSNER FLYNN   FOREWORD BY ICHTHYOLOGIST DR. PHILLIP S. LOBEL

NATIONAL
GEOGRAPHIC
KiDS

WASHINGTON, D.C.

TABLE OF CONTENTS

A reef shark in the Caribbean Sea swims over a coral reef.

FOREWORD

My own experience with sharks began while volunteering at the Cleveland Aquarium in Ohio as a freshman in high school. It was fascinating to help feed small sharks and help keep them alive in an aquarium environment. That led me to join the aquarium's expeditions in the Florida Keys during summers. I knew then that I wanted to be an ichthyologist—a biologist who studies fish.

In college, I worked at the University of Hawai'i marine lab at Enewetak Atoll during school breaks and summers. There were lots of sharks in those days, and one of my dive jobs was to chase away sharks from the professors trying to do underwater surveys and collections. I am now a professor myself, and I've studied sharks and other fish around the world for 50 years. I have seen, firsthand, the negative impacts on sharks from overfishing and polluted waters. I have also seen the positive recovery in several places due to the efforts of local dive shops that want to help preserve the ocean. Sharks are very resilient and incredibly tough physically, but they reproduce relatively slowly. There is hope for ecological recovery, but we still must do better to protect sharks and all marine life.

The facts you will read in this book have come from hundreds of years of observations and scientific research. Yet there are many aspects of shark behavior that are very hard to study in the wild. The home range of individual sharks and rays needs to be mapped in order to better determine the size of marine protective areas. This is where new powerful technologies can be used, like a data-collecting tag about the size of a watch that can be placed on a wild shark. These new tools are needed for us to learn what sharks are really doing out in the deep blue ocean. New biological tools—such as testing DNA to determine the relationships of sharks and other animals—change the way we think about the relationships of animals and their population.

Conservation successes thanks to these new technologies also bring new challenges to society. For example, the increase of seals and of great white sharks that eat the seals around Cape Cod, Massachusetts, is a result of good conservation management for the recovery of the great white shark, which was once endangered. But this now poses increased risks to humans who swim off what were once "safe" beaches. New technologies and a better understanding of shark behavior will be needed to meet the challenge of managing the safety of both wildlife and humans.

This book is a huge collection of neat facts about sharks. But there is much more to learn! I hope it inspires you to learn the mysteries of the ocean and its creatures—and maybe even to get in the water as a snorkeler or scuba diver yourself and see whale sharks, reef sharks, and stingrays up close and in person!

Phillip S. Lobel, Ph.D.
Professor of Biology, Boston University
MCZ Associate in Ichthyology, Harvard University

FACTS, FIGURES, AND COMMON NAMES
In this book, you'll find 1,000 facts about sharks and their relatives. At the back you'll find a glossary, which provides definitions of special words and terms used in the book. There is also a summary of the many different types of sharks and their main characteristics. Common names rather than the scientific Latin names of sharks are used, but note that some species have several common names. These alternative names may be used by some of the resources listed at the back of the book.

7

10 FAST FACTS

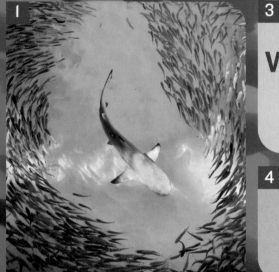

1

All sharks are FISH.

2

SOME SHARKS ARE **APEX PREDATORS**, WHICH MEANS THEY ARE AT THE **TOP OF THEIR FOOD CHAIN.**

3

SHARKS COME IN A **VARIETY OF COLORS,** FROM GRAY TO BLACK TO BUBBLEGUM PINK.

4

Most sharks live in OCEANS. Some live in FRESHWATER rivers.

5

SHARKS ARE CARTILAGINOUS, WHICH MEANS THEY HAVE A SKELETON MADE OF CARTILAGE INSTEAD OF BONE.

ABOUT SHARKS

6

SHARKS ARE HEAVIER THAN SEAWATER SO THEY MUST SWIM CONSTANTLY TO AVOID SINKING TO THE OCEAN FLOOR.

8 Some sharks are so small they can fit in the PALM OF YOUR HAND. Others are longer than a BUS.

10 A small number of sharks, like the salmon shark, are WARM-BLOODED. They can CONTROL THEIR BODY TEMPERATURE.

7 Most sharks are COLD-BLOODED— their body temperature changes with that of the surrounding water.

9 There are about 500 different species of sharks.

a group of hammerhead sharks

SHARK HABITATS

Sharks swim in all the oceans—and in some freshwater lakes and rivers—around the world. In the oceans, some species swim in deep waters near the ocean floor and far from land, while others hang out in the shallows of coastal regions. Here's a look at fascinating examples of sharks from 10 different locations across the globe.

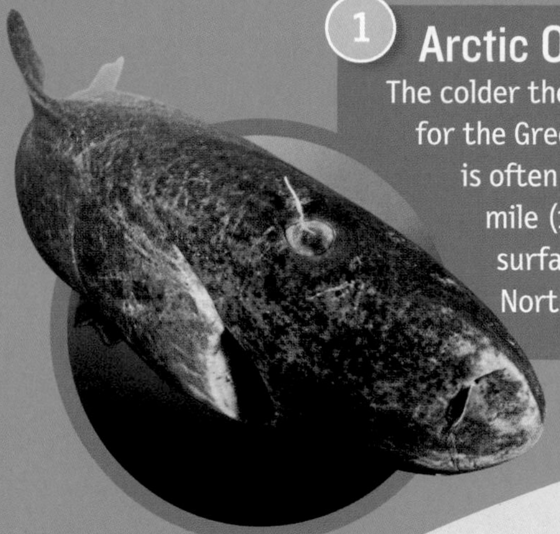

1 Arctic Ocean

The colder the water, the better for the Greenland shark, which is often seen more than a mile (1.6 km) below the surface in the Arctic and North Atlantic Oceans.

2 Hawai'i

Although rarely seen in the wild, the megamouth shark was first discovered off the coast of Hawai'i, U.S.A., and has been spotted swimming near Indonesia.

3 South America

The tiger shark—named for the dark bars that run down the bodies of juveniles—can be seen in tropical and subtropical waters, such as those near parts of South America, plus the Gulf of Mexico and the Caribbean Sea.

4 Atlantic Ocean

Known for its yellowish-brown skin, the lemon shark can be found throughout the Atlantic Ocean, from the coast of New Jersey, U.S.A., to Brazil in South America.

ARCTIC

1

NORTH AMERICA

ATLANTIC OCEAN

Hawai'i U.S.A.

Gulf of Mexico

New Jersey U.S.A.

Caribbean Sea

4

2

3

Brazil

PACIFIC OCEAN

SOUTH AMERICA

SOUTHERN

Europe

5
Inhabiting cool waters around the globe, the blue shark is one of the main species around Europe, including in the Mediterranean Sea. It regularly swims between the ocean's surface and waters about 1,900 feet (580 m) deep.

Asia

6
The broadnose sevengill—a kind of cow shark—lives offshore in great numbers in the Indian and Pacific Oceans. In shallows around Asia, it is one of the most common shark predators.

Indian Ocean

7
Zebra sharks have a range that stretches from the eastern coast of Africa to the eastern coast of Australia, an area that spans the Indian Ocean. Bottom-dwellers, these sharks spend their time in coastal areas and hunt for ocean animals that hide in reefs and rocks.

Southeast Africa

8
The whale shark is highly migratory. Among its hot spots are the warm waters off southeastern Africa, including along the shores of Mozambique and Madagascar.

New Guinea

9
The epaulette shark, which uses its fins to "walk" on land and on the seafloor, typically hangs out in coral reefs and tide pools off northern Australia and New Guinea.

Australia

10
The great hammerhead shark hangs out in shallow waters along the eastern, western, and northern coasts of Australia.

OCEAN

EUROPE

5

Mediterranean Sea

ASIA

6

AFRICA

INDIAN OCEAN

Mozambique

Madagascar

8

Indonesia

New Guinea

7

9

10

PACIFIC OCEAN

AUSTRALIA

MAP KEY
- Polar waters
- Temperate waters
- Tropical and subtropical waters

OCEAN

ANTARCTICA

1 All living things on Earth are classified into **SEVEN CATEGORIES**— kingdom, phylum, class, order, family, genus, and species.

2 This science of **NAMING, DEFINING, AND CLASSIFYING GROUPS** of living things is known as **TAXONOMY**.

3 ALL SHARKS—AND ALL ANIMALS ON THE PLANET—ARE PART OF **KINGDOM ANIMALIA**.

4 A **phylum** IS A GROUP THAT SHARES SIMILAR CHARACTERISTICS. SHARKS BELONG TO PHYLUM **Chordata** AND SUBPHYLUM **Vertebrata**.

5 Vertebrata, known commonly as **VERTEBRATES**, are animals with a **SPINAL CORD** and a **BACKBONE**.

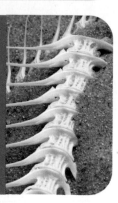

25 CLASSIFIED FACTS ABOUT THE

6 A **spinal cord** is the large group of nerves running through the center of the spine. It carries **messages** between the **brain** and the rest of the body.

7 Sharks are part of **CLASS CHONDRICHTHYES**, one of two groups of **CARTILAGINOUS** fish—or those with a skeleton of flexible cartilage, not bone.

8 **"CHONDRICHTHYES"** comes from two **ANCIENT GREEK WORDS** meaning "cartilage" and "fish."

9 THE **CLASS CHONDRICHTHYES** IS DIVIDED INTO TWO SUBCLASSES— HOLOCEPHALI AND ELASMOBRANCHII.

10 There are about 1,000 species of elasmobranchs, which include **SHARKS, SKATES, RAYS,** and **CHIMAERAS**.

11 Some 40 species of chimaeras make up the **HOLOCEPHALI** subclass.

12 **"HOLOCEPHALI"** MEANS **"WHOLE HEAD,"** A NOD TO THE CHIMAERA'S ABNORMALLY LARGE NOGGIN.

13 *Elasmos* is Greek for "metal plate" and *branchii* is Latin for "gills," a fish's breathing organs. Together, this name refers to the shark's **visible gill slits.**

14 Elasmobranchii is further divided into two **SUPERORDERS— SELACHII,** the sharks, and **BATOIDEA,** the skates and rays.

15 Scientists have organized all sharks into **EIGHT ORDERS** based on sets of **COMMON FEATURES.**

16 The eight orders are angel sharks, carpet sharks, dogfish sharks, frilled and cow sharks, mackerel sharks, bullhead sharks, saw sharks, and ground sharks.

17 **ANGEL SHARKS ARE EASILY IDENTIFIED BY THEIR FLAT BODIES AND WINGLIKE FINS.**

18 **CARPET SHARKS** have **PATTERNED SKIN** that can **RESEMBLE SOME CARPETS.**

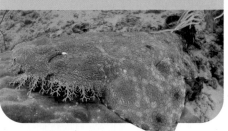

SHARK FAMILY

19 **DOGFISH SHARKS** have **LONG SNOUTS** with **SHORT MOUTHS** and five pairs of gills. They **TRAVEL AND HUNT IN PACKS** like dogs!

20 **FRILLED SHARKS** AND **COW SHARKS** UNIQUELY HAVE SIX OR SEVEN PAIRS OF GILLS. MOST SHARKS HAVE ONLY FIVE.

21 MACKEREL SHARKS have LONG SNOUTS and MOUTHS, with five pairs of gills.

22 **Bullhead sharks** LIVE IN **warm, tropical** WATERS AND HAVE **hornlike** RIDGES OVER THEIR EYES.

23 SAW SHARKS have long, flat snouts studded with teeth that look like CHAIN SAW BLADES.

24 **GROUND SHARKS** have wide mouths with sharp-edged teeth.

25 There are more ground shark species—over 270—than any other order of sharks.

13

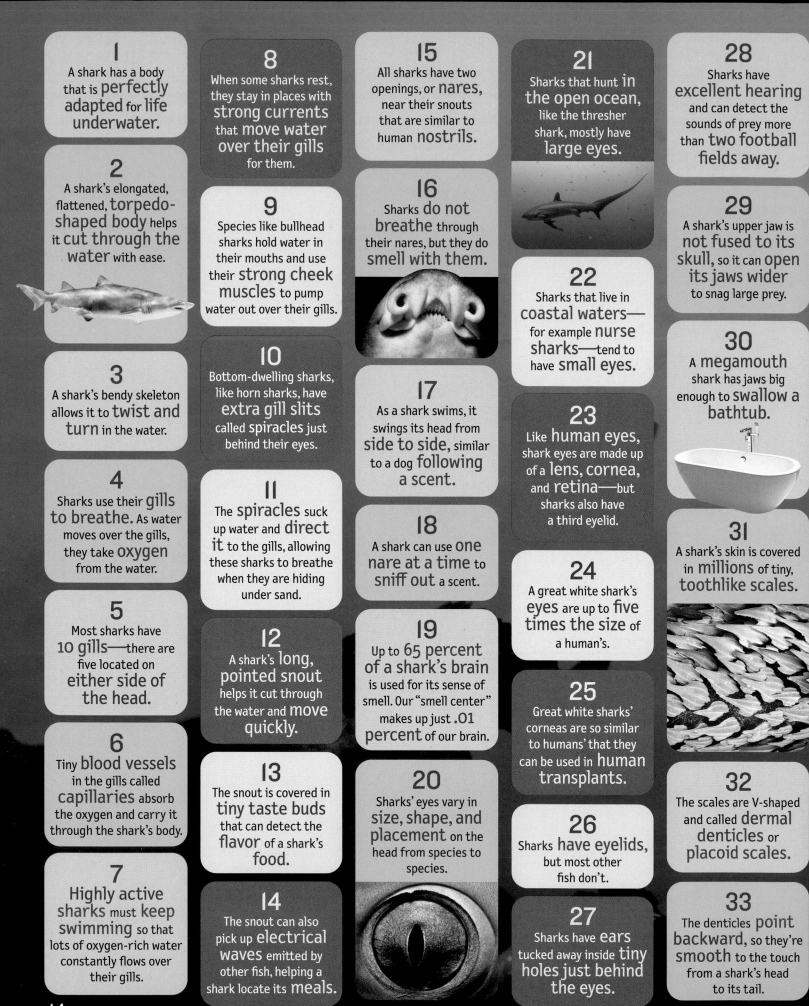

1
A shark has a body that is perfectly adapted for life underwater.

2
A shark's elongated, flattened, torpedo-shaped body helps it cut through the water with ease.

3
A shark's bendy skeleton allows it to twist and turn in the water.

4
Sharks use their gills to breathe. As water moves over the gills, they take oxygen from the water.

5
Most sharks have 10 gills—there are five located on either side of the head.

6
Tiny blood vessels in the gills called capillaries absorb the oxygen and carry it through the shark's body.

7
Highly active sharks must keep swimming so that lots of oxygen-rich water constantly flows over their gills.

8
When some sharks rest, they stay in places with strong currents that move water over their gills for them.

9
Species like bullhead sharks hold water in their mouths and use their strong cheek muscles to pump water out over their gills.

10
Bottom-dwelling sharks, like horn sharks, have extra gill slits called spiracles just behind their eyes.

11
The spiracles suck up water and direct it to the gills, allowing these sharks to breathe when they are hiding under sand.

12
A shark's long, pointed snout helps it cut through the water and move quickly.

13
The snout is covered in tiny taste buds that can detect the flavor of a shark's food.

14
The snout can also pick up electrical waves emitted by other fish, helping a shark locate its meals.

15
All sharks have two openings, or nares, near their snouts that are similar to human nostrils.

16
Sharks do not breathe through their nares, but they do smell with them.

17
As a shark swims, it swings its head from side to side, similar to a dog following a scent.

18
A shark can use one nare at a time to sniff out a scent.

19
Up to 65 percent of a shark's brain is used for its sense of smell. Our "smell center" makes up just .01 percent of our brain.

20
Sharks' eyes vary in size, shape, and placement on the head from species to species.

21
Sharks that hunt in the open ocean, like the thresher shark, mostly have large eyes.

22
Sharks that live in coastal waters—for example nurse sharks—tend to have small eyes.

23
Like human eyes, shark eyes are made up of a lens, cornea, and retina—but sharks also have a third eyelid.

24
A great white shark's eyes are up to five times the size of a human's.

25
Great white sharks' corneas are so similar to humans' that they can be used in human transplants.

26
Sharks have eyelids, but most other fish don't.

27
Sharks have ears tucked away inside tiny holes just behind the eyes.

28
Sharks have excellent hearing and can detect the sounds of prey more than two football fields away.

29
A shark's upper jaw is not fused to its skull, so it can open its jaws wider to snag large prey.

30
A megamouth shark has jaws big enough to swallow a bathtub.

31
A shark's skin is covered in millions of tiny, toothlike scales.

32
The scales are V-shaped and called dermal denticles or placoid scales.

33
The denticles point backward, so they're smooth to the touch from a shark's head to its tail.

34
If you rub a shark's skin from **tail to head,** the denticles are as **rough as sandpaper.**

35
Dermal denticles help **reduce drag** from the water, allowing for a **swifter swim.**

36
The hard denticles **protect a shark's skin** when it **scrapes against coral reefs** and rocks.

37
The silky shark gets its name from its **extra-small denticles,** which give it a **silky feel** to the touch.

38
As a shark **grows,** new denticles fill gaps in its skin and replace **old or lost ones.**

39
Sharks have **nerve endings embedded** in their skin that are sensitive to touch.

40
Most sharks have a **small tongue,** which connects muscles in their jaws.

41
All sharks have **several fins** that help them keep their **balance** and **stay upright** while they swim.

42
A shark **swishes its tail** from side to side to pick up **speed** and **propel its body** forward.

43
A shark's **caudal fin,** or **tail fin,** has an **upper lobe** and a **lower lobe,** which help the shark propel itself through **water.**

44
On the **fastest sharks,** like shortfin makos and salmon sharks, **these two lobes are similar in size.**

45
The **tail fin lobes** of slower sharks, like basking sharks, are **different sizes.**

46
More than half of a **shark's mass** is muscle.

47
Unlike most fish, sharks do not have a gas-filled **swim bladder** to help them stay afloat.

48
A shark's **fat-filled liver** helps it float and stores **energy for body processes.**

49
The **heart** of a whale shark weighs more than 40 pounds (18 kg). That's **80 times** heavier than your heart!

50
A shark's heart has **two blood-filled chambers.** A human heart has four.

a blacktip reef shark swimming in shallow water

50 Facts About SHARK ANATOMY

❶ All sharks have **four kinds of fins**—dorsal (on the back), pectoral and pelvic (on the underside), and caudal (tail).

❷ A shark's fins appear **rigid**—but can **curl, lift,** and **lower.**

❸ Fins help sharks stay **stable** and move **through the water.**

❹ Sharks also use their **fins to communicate.** Male sharks often bite a **female's pectoral fin to show interest.**

❺ A shark has **two dorsal fins**—a large one **near the front** of its body and a smaller one located near **the tail.**

❻ When a shark is near the ocean's surface, its **large, front dorsal** fin sticks out of the water.

❼ Dorsal fins can be used as **fast-acting rudders** to help sharks make **quick and sudden turns.**

A great white shark uses its fins to leap out of the water to catch a seal.

SHARK FINS

8 A fully grown great white shark's front **dorsal fin** is about 3.2 feet (1 m) tall—**that's taller than a four-year-old child!**

9 Scars and notches caused by parasite bites and other types of trauma can make a shark's dorsal fins look like **tattered flags.**

10 The **fins** of each species of shark are **unique** in shape. Researchers use this to help identify shark species in the wild.

11 Sharks have a pair of **pectoral fins** that help them steer and move up and down while they swim.

12 Nurse sharks use their pair of **pectoral fins** as legs to **walk** along the **ocean floor.**

13 The **caudal fin** comes in different shapes and sizes.

14 The caudal fin of the **zebra shark** is almost **as long as its body.**

15 Pelvic fins prevent a shark from **rolling to the left or the right.**

1 Sharks have HUNDREDS of teeth, arranged in layered rows. If any break off, NEW, SHARP teeth take their place.

2 SCIENTISTS THINK SHARKS' TEETH **EVOLVED** FROM **SCALES** COVERING THEIR **LIPS.**

3 Sharks have between 2 and 15 rows of teeth. Only the outer one or two are put to use.

4 A shark's back rows of teeth act as replacements. They **MOVE FORWARD** as older, front-row teeth **WEAR DOWN** or are lost.

5 Sharks NEVER STOP growing teeth.

25 SHARP FACTS ABOUT

6 SHARK TEETH ARE attached TO THE skin COVERING THE JAW, not rooted beneath gums LIKE HUMAN TEETH.

7 Because they're **LOOSELY ATTACHED** to the skin, sharks' teeth easily **FALL OUT** or get stuck in prey as they bite down.

8 On average, a shark loses about 20 teeth **PER WEEK.** That's up to 30,000 teeth in its lifetime.

9 It takes 8 to 10 DAYS for a NEW TOOTH to grow in a shark's mouth.

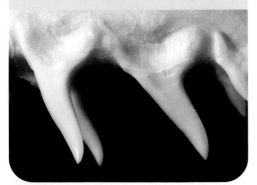

10 Younger SHARKS replace their teeth MORE OFTEN, SINCE THEY'RE MORE ACTIVELY FEEDING TO GROW.

11 With teeth up to **TWO INCHES (5 CM)** tall, a fully grown white shark has the **LARGEST TEETH** of any living shark.

12 SHARKS are born with COMPLETE SETS of teeth.

13 The hard **OUTER LAYER** of sharks' teeth is known as **ENAMELOID**.

14 A **BULL SHARK** has **ABOUT 50 TEETH** in each of its **SEVEN ROWS**.

15 SCIENTISTS CAN **IDENTIFY** MANY SPECIES OF SHARKS BY THEIR TEETH.

16

A **WHALE SHARK** has about 3,000 **TINY TEETH** that are each a half inch (13 mm) long.

17 Predatory sharks have teeth that are **POINTED** with **JAGGED EDGES**, designed to **SLICE**, rip, or tear food.

SHARK TEETH

18

18

A **GREAT WHITE SHARK'S** teeth are **SERRATED** like a **STEAK KNIFE**, allowing it to tear apart **LARGE PREY** such as seals and sea lions.

19 If its prey is **TOO BIG** to eat in one bite, a shark **BITES DOWN** and shakes its head back and forth to **RIP OFF** pieces.

25 Sharks' teeth **LAST LONGER** in the **COLDER** months, because that's when their prey are **LESS ACTIVE**.

20 **BOTTOM-FEEDER** SHARKS USE THEIR **THICK, FLATTENED** TEETH TO FEED ON SHELLFISH AND SEA URCHINS.

21 **FRILLED SHARKS HAVE 300 ROWS OF NEEDLELIKE** TEETH.

23

Some shark species' teeth are made out of natural **FLUORIDE**, a main ingredient in **TOOTHPASTE**.

22 The **COOKIECUTTER** shark loses and **REGROWS** its lower teeth in complete rows, not one at a time.

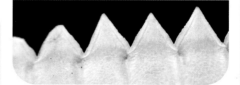

24 The **FLUORIDE** protects shark teeth from **ACID** produced by **BACTERIA**.

1 Sharks began to **evolve** before dinosaurs walked on Earth, hundreds of **millions of years** before **humans** lived.

2 Since then, shark features have changed and **adapted** to make them the **strongest animals** in the ocean.

3 Adaptations such as **flexible jaws,** a **muscular tail,** and **highly advanced senses** have helped sharks survive for so long.

4 Sharks **pass down** these adaptations from **generation to generation** through their **genes,** made of DNA.

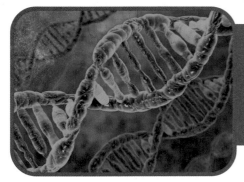

5 DNA—the blueprint of life—is the material that carries all the **information** about how a living thing will **look** and **function.**

6 Sharks leave their DNA in **ocean water** through flecks of **skin and scales** and bits of **mucus and waste** released from their bodies. Scientists can use it to learn what's living in a patch of water.

7 Scientists recently completed the **genome map** of a great white shark—a look at its entire **genetic makeup** and **DNA.**

SHARK GENES

A shark embryo in its egg case. The embryo contains genes from its parents.

8 Great whites have **41 pairs of chromo-somes**, each made of DNA, compared to humans' **23 pairs.**

9 Great white sharks also have **special genes** that help them **heal faster** and may protect them from **cancer.**

10 Researchers plan to **study shark genes** to pick up on clues about how humans can **fight cancer.**

11 Scientists say great whites have more genes devoted to **blood clotting** and **wound-healing** than any other fish, or any bird or mammal.

12 According to recent research, **elephant sharks** have several genes that are **nearly identical** to those in humans.

13 Experts are studying **DNA** from Greenland sharks, the **longest living vertebrates** on the planet, to learn how humans can **live longer.**

14 Experts often use DNA found in **sharks' teeth** to identify **different species.**

15 DNA from a **tooth fragment** retrieved from a surfer's foot **25 years** after a **shark bite** was matched to a **blacktip shark.**

15 RECORD-BREAKING

1 The length of a long **city bus** and weighing up to 75,000 pounds (34,000 kg), the whale shark is the **world's largest shark**—and fish.

2 The **Greenland shark**, the **world's slowest-swimming shark**, cruises at an average speed of about .76 mile an hour (1.2 km/h).

3 **Basking sharks** are the largest shark pups, measuring roughly 5 feet 7 inches (1.7 m) at birth. That's longer than a **10-year-old** is tall.

4 The **dusky shark** has the most **powerful bite** among sharks. The force is twice that of a human's bite.

5 Regularly swimming at speeds of **30 miles an hour (50 km/h)**, a shortfin mako is the **world's fastest shark**.

6 Shorter than a **playing card** at birth and a table tennis paddle as an adult, the **dwarf lanternshark** is the **tiniest shark**.

7 **Dogfish** generally can live **70 years** or more, which is longer than the average life span of other shark orders.

Sharks circle a shoal of small fish. Sharks reach their greatest speeds when chasing prey.

FACTS ABOUT SHARKS

8 The velvet belly lanternshark is among the world's **deepest dwellers**, typically found almost **half a mile** (0.8 km) beneath the **ocean's surface**.

9 Frilled sharks **carry their babies** for more than three years before giving birth—the **longest pregnancy** of all vertebrates.

10 A **thresher shark's** tail is as **long as its body**—proportionately the **longest tail** among all sharks.

11 The **great white shark**—the **largest predatory fish** on Earth—can swallow an **adult seal** in one bite.

12 An adult **great hammerhead shark** has been recorded **swallowing whole** an **80-pound** (36.3-kg) adult blacktip shark.

13 A team of scientists in **Polynesia** once spotted a group of **700 sharks swimming together**—among the **largest school** of sharks ever observed.

14 Experts tracked a **whale shark** across more than 12,000 miles (19,300 km) of ocean. That's the **longest** migration ever recorded for the species.

15 In relation to the size of its jaws, a **cookiecutter shark** has the **biggest teeth** of any shark.

23

1 Angel sharks get their name from the **ELEGANT WAY** they glide through the water.

2 THE SPECIES' **PECTORAL** FINS **LOOK LIKE WINGS,** ADDING TO THEIR **ANGELIC** APPEARANCE.

3 All 23 species of angel sharks often use their winglike fins to **STEER** through the water.

4 MOST ANGEL SHARKS ARE ABOUT five feet (1.5 m) LONG AND CAN WEIGH AROUND 60 pounds (27 kg).

5 Angel sharks are found in TEMPERATE to TROPICAL-TEMPERATE waters along the coast of every continent EXCEPT ANTARCTICA.

25 GRACEFUL FACTS ABOUT

6 Angel sharks are **NOCTURNAL,** spending most of their day **BURIED** in the seabed, often with only their eyes sticking out.

7 Unlike most sharks, an angel shark's **EYES** are on **TOP OF ITS HEAD**—all the better to spot prey when hanging out at the **BOTTOM OF THE OCEAN.**

8 Angel sharks tend to hang out in flat, **SANDY** areas between **ROCKS** near **REEFS** or **KELP FORESTS** where there are **PLENTY** of fish.

9 Angel sharks **AMBUSH** their prey by **DARTING FORWARD** from their hiding spots to grab unsuspecting animals.

10 ATLANTIC ANGEL SHARKS ARE ALSO CALLED **SAND DEVILS** FOR THEIR SNEAKY HUNTING TACTICS.

11 Their **FAVORITE FOODS** to munch on? **MOLLUSKS, CRABS,** and **SMALL FISH.**

12 **ANGEL SHARKS** TAKE ABOUT **ONE-TENTH OF A SECOND TO SNAG A SNACK.**

13 Some angel shark species **MAY WAIT WEEKS** on the ocean floor until the **RIGHT MEAL,** such as a crab, comes along.

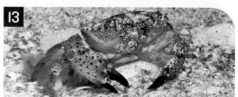

14 Angel sharks have barbels, or **WHISKERS,** near their mouth, which they use to **DETECT PREY.**

15 The **JAPANESE** angel shark is the largest of the species, and grows to be nearly **SEVEN FEET (2.1 M)** in length.

16 A **MOM** ANGEL SHARK TYPICALLY GIVES BIRTH TO **LITTERS** OF 8 TO 25 BABIES, OR **PUPS.**

18 Because of their flat **BODIES** and wide **FINS,** angel sharks are often **CONFUSED** with rays.

17 Angel shark **PUPS** are about as big as an iPAD when they're **BORN.**

ANGEL SHARKS

19 Unlike angel sharks, rays don't have **barbels,** and some have a long tail with a **sharp barb** that they use for protection.

20 In the **WILD,** angel sharks can live for up to **35 YEARS.**

22 The **SAWBACK** angel shark has a row of **THORNS** running along the **MIDDLE** of its back.

21 In the dark of the night, angel sharks can use the **BIOLUMINESCENCE** of jellyfish and other kinds of **PLANKTON** to help spot their prey.

25 The largest population of angel sharks is close to the **CANARY ISLANDS,** where the sharks swim in **PROTECTED WATERS.**

23 After sawfish, angel sharks are the most threatened of all sharks, due to **OVERFISHING** and **HABITAT LOSS.**

24 Nearly HALF of all species of angel sharks are considered CRITICALLY ENDANGERED.

15 WHOPPING FACTS ABOUT

① **One** whale shark weighs as much as **five adult male African elephants.**

② A **newborn whale shark** is only 25 inches (64 cm) long—about the size of a **kid's skateboard.**

③ A whale shark's **mouth opens** to a span of about four and a half feet (1.4 m)—almost **the width of a car.**

④ Despite their huge size, whale sharks don't gobble their prey. They prefer to feed slowly on tiny **fish** and **plankton.**

⑤ A whale shark sucks up **gallons of water** in its massive mouth, using bristly rods inside its throat to **filter out the food.**

⑥ A whale shark eats up to **two tons** (2.2 t) of **plankton** every day.

⑦ Whale sharks are curious creatures and often **swim up to boats** and **scuba divers** to get a closer look.

close-up of a whale shark

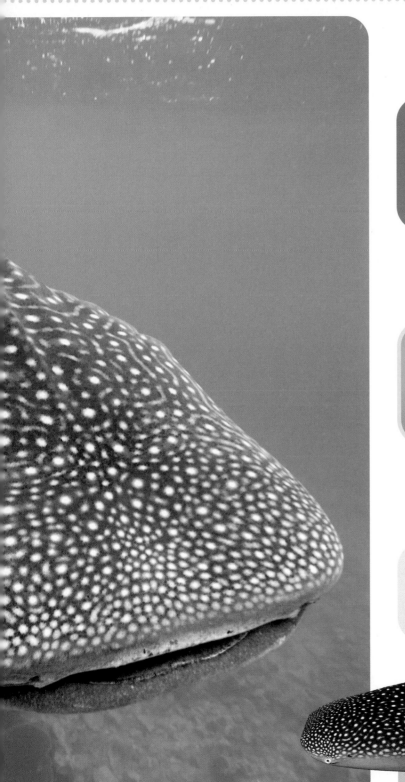

8 Whale sharks are **not speedy.** They travel at an average pace of about **three miles an hour (5 km/h).**

9 Still, they do get around: Some whale sharks swim **6,200 miles (9,980 km)** or more each year.

10 Scientists have found the DNA of specific whale sharks in the Caribbean Sea, the Indian Ocean, and the Pacific Ocean—showing just how **much the fish travel.**

11 The pattern of **stripes and dots** on each whale shark's skin is unique, which helps **identify them.**

12 When feeding, whale sharks spend most of their time swimming within **100 feet (30 m)** of the ocean's surface.

13 A marine biologist once observed a whale shark at a depth of **6,324 feet (1,928 m).**

14 In the wild, whale sharks have a **life span** of about 70 years.

15 The whale shark was **first identified as a species** by a scientist in South Africa in 1828.

27

75 FIERCE FACTS ABOUT SHARK HUNTING AND FEEDING

1 Sharks play a big role in balancing ocean biodiversity by keeping the numbers of prey animals in check.

2 ONE OF THE TOP PREDATORS OF A SHARK IS ANOTHER SHARK.

3 Some small young sharks are eaten by larger bony fish.

4 Researchers in a submersible some 1,475 feet (450 m) below the surface of the Atlantic saw a dogfish shark being eaten whole by a large grouper fish.

5 Sharks tend to be selective eaters, each species going after a particular range of prey.

6 By eating injured, dying, or dead animals, sharks keep the oceans clean and prevent fish diseases from spreading.

7 While some sharks feed frantically and others slowly, nearly all of them are hunters.

8 Sharks are light eaters relative to their body weight.

9 Sharks eat about 2 percent of their body weight at each meal—less than the average person.

10 A nine-foot (2.7-m)-long sand tiger shark that weighs 289 pounds (131 kg) may eat just 10 pounds (4.5 kg) of food in a week.

11 To compare, adult humans eat about 38 pounds (17 kg) of food each week.

12 If their main source of prey is low, sharks can switch to another food source.

13 Most sharks feed primarily on smaller fish and invertebrates.

14 LARGE SHARK SPECIES PREY MOSTLY ON SEALS, SEA LIONS, AND OTHER MARINE MAMMALS.

15 Many sharks go after weak, sick, or dying prey because they're easier to catch.

16 Sometimes, a bunch of sharks will fight for the same prey at the same time, also known as a feeding frenzy.

sharks circling above prey, ready to feed

17 When it feeds on shellfish, a bonnethead shark accidentally eats lots of seagrass and other leafy greens found in the ocean.

18 Young bonnethead sharks, still learning how to feed, are believed to accidentally eat more greens than the adults.

19 Silky sharks are known to rocket through schools of fish, gobbling them up as they go.

20 GREAT WHITES HUNT BY SURPRISING THEIR PREY FROM BELOW AND DISABLING THEM WITH ONE MASSIVE BITE.

21 When a great white shark bites its prey, its eyes roll back into its head. This protects the eyes in case the prey fights back.

22 Great whites are known to take a sample bite out of curiosity. If they don't like the taste, they'll swim off.

23 Aggressive hunters, hammerheads are thought of as some of the most advanced predators in the ocean.

24 Hammerheads use their wide heads to pin stingrays against the seafloor before biting them.

25 Thresher sharks have a tall, bladelike tail that can be as long as the rest of their body, which they sling over their heads to smash smaller fish.

26 ONE THRESHER SHARK WAS ABLE TO SLING ITS TAIL UP TO 80 MILES AN HOUR (129 KM/H) TO ATTACK ITS PREY.

27 Cookiecutter sharks bite chunks more than 20 times their body weight from whales and seals.

28 Cookiecutter sharks are also known to take bites out of the rubber domes of nuclear submarines.

29 To feed, cookiecutter sharks use their "lips" for suction and teeth for drilling into their victims' flesh.

30 Once attached, the cookiecutter spins its body and uses its sharp teeth to take a cookie-shaped bite of its prey.

31 To catch prey, a shortfin mako leaps 20 feet (6 m) above the water surface—that's taller than a giraffe!

32 BLACKTIP REEF SHARKS HERD SCHOOLS OF FISH INTO TIGHT BALLS BEFORE GOING IN FOR THE KILL.

33 Greenland sharks eat seabirds and dead whales.

34 Greenland sharks are also known to snatch caribou standing near holes in the ice.

35 The remains of horses and parts of a polar bear have been found inside a deceased Greenland shark's stomach.

36 Tiger sharks gobble up fish, other sharks, seabirds, iguanas, sea turtles, and even garbage and dead animals.

37 Researchers and fishers have found everything from license plates to boat cushions in the bellies of sharks.

38 Tiger sharks have curved, pointy, and supersharp teeth that can puncture turtle shells.

39 To find prey, a nurse shark uses its snout to root through the sand.

40 Nurse sharks hunt at night so they can sneak up on unsuspecting, sleeping sea creatures.

41 Nurse sharks use their strong jaws like a vacuum, to suck up food.

42 The sucking noise may sound like a nursing baby—one source for the name nurse sharks.

43 Sand tiger sharks fill their bellies with air to float and stay still while watching for prey.

44 Saw sharks use their long, spiky, swordlike snouts to dig up crustaceans and smaller fish to eat.

45 Saw sharks can also slap and stun their prey with their unique snouts.

46 After a big meal, an oceanic whitetip shark can go for up to a month before eating again.

47 The majority of sharks can survive for six weeks or more without food.

48 A swell shark living in captivity once went 15 months without eating—the longest time period observed among sharks.

49 Blue sharks are known to grab fishing lines and swim away with their stolen snacks.

50 To catch a meal, a spinner shark takes a spinning leap out of the water before crashing back down on its prey.

51 A SPINNER SHARK'S TINY TEETH ARE NOT SHARP ENOUGH TO TEAR INTO FLESH, SO IT TYPICALLY SWALLOWS ITS PREY WHOLE.

52 The six-foot (1.8 m)-long frilled shark can swallow eels up to three feet (0.9 m) long.

53 A frilled shark's white teeth contrast well against its dark skin, which may attract prey right to its mouth.

54 Frilled sharks appear to close their gill slits to create suction, which helps them capture food in their mouths.

55 Frilled sharks sometimes surprise their prey by curving their body like a spring, then launching forward, snakelike, with a quick strike.

56 When biting, a shark can drop its upper and lower jaw and rotate the teeth outward, allowing a larger bite or better suction to capture prey.

57 An attacking goblin shark shoots both its flexible jaws outward, trapping prey in its mouth before impaling it on its jagged teeth.

58 KNOWN AS SLINGSHOT FEEDING, THIS BEHAVIOR IS UNIQUE TO GOBLIN SHARKS.

59 A horn shark uses its super-strong bite to crack open rock-hard mollusk shells.

60 Horn sharks' spines turn purple when they eat a lot of purple sea urchins.

61 Sharks are sometimes called "wolves of the sea" because of some species' habit of gathering in packs when it's time to hunt.

62 A pack of some 15 dusky sharks was once spotted devouring a humpback whale off the coast of South Africa.

63 When hunting a seal, broadnose sevengill sharks uniquely form a pack and surround the animal to catch it.

64 These team tactics help broadnose sevengills catch big, fast prey like dolphins.

65 Sand tiger sharks that swarm around schools of fish take turns to gobble up as much prey as they can.

66 Thresher sharks work in pairs to round up fish and stun them with a whip of their tails.

67 Sometimes, great white sharks swim on their backs as they approach prey.

68 The reason for this predatory move—known as the inverted approach—is unclear.

69 WHEN GREAT WHITES HUNT SEALS, THEY DO SO ESPECIALLY AT DAWN AND DUSK, WHEN THESE MAMMALS ARE MOST ACTIVE.

70 Some experts think great white sharks may work together to bring down larger prey such as whales.

71 When hunting from below, great whites rely on the sunlight to make out prey swimming close to the surface.

72 Scientists once saw a 13-foot (4-m)-long great white launching itself from the water to snag a seal.

73 It was the first time a "breach feeding" by sharks had been documented at night.

74 Whitetip reef sharks will wriggle through tiny cracks in a coral reef to chase prey.

75 Since sharks evolved millions of years before humans existed, people are not part of their historical diets.

29

1 A deep layer of the ocean—starting about 3,300 feet (1,000 m) down—is called the **MIDNIGHT ZONE** because it gets **NO SUNLIGHT**.

2 Just above this is the **TWILIGHT ZONE**— from 650 feet (198 m) down— which is less **MURKY** but visibility is still limited.

3 Some **40 PERCENT** of the 500 or so species of **SHARKS** live in these two zones.

4 There's very **LITTLE VEGETATION** in the deep ocean, since the sunlight there is **TOO WEAK** for most plants to grow.

5 Deep-sea sharks eat **DEAD ANIMALS** that fall from the surface, or **OTHER CREATURES** that live down there.

6 Cookiecutter sharks are found deep in the twilight zone during the day, but they swim to **SHALLOWER WATER** at night to **HUNT**.

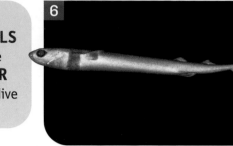

25 IN-DEPTH FACTS ABOUT DEEP-SEA

7 IN PART DUE TO LESS AVAILABLE FOOD, DEEP-SEA SHARKS MATURE MORE SLOWLY THAN OTHER SHARKS, AND PRODUCE FEWER OFFSPRING.

8 Deep-sea sharks have unique— even bizarre—**ADAPTATIONS** for living in their cold and dark environments.

9 The sharks rely especially on their keen sense of **SMELL** to help them navigate the pitch-black waters.

10 The snout of a goblin shark— which lives in the midnight zone—is covered in tiny **ELECTROSENSORS** that help it feel for prey in the **DARK**.

11 The goblin shark's unusually **LARGE** and **BULGY SNOUT** also boosts its ability to **SNIFF OUT** prey.

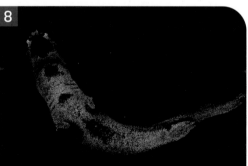

12 Some deep-sea shark species have **TRANSPARENT PATCHES** of skin above their eyes that experts think **HELP THEM SEE** what's lurking above.

13 Blackbelly lanternsharks have **GLOWING DOTS** along the length of their bodies, allowing them to **FIND ONE ANOTHER** in the deep.

14 Some deep-sea species of sharks have **OVERSIZE EYES** to pick up **TRACES OF LIGHT.**

15 THE RARELY SEEN BLUNTNOSE SIXGILL IS A DEEP-SEA SHARK WITH A **HUGE, OILY LIVER** THAT HELPS IT FLOAT.

17 BECAUSE OF THIS LARGE SIZE, BLUNTNOSE SIXGILLS ARE ALSO KNOWN AS **COW SHARKS.**

16 In 2019, a **20-FOOT (6.1-M)-LONG** bluntnose sixgill was found that **WEIGHED MORE THAN A TON (0.9 T).**

18 The giant false catshark swims at depths of about **4,900 FEET (1,500 M).**

SHARKS

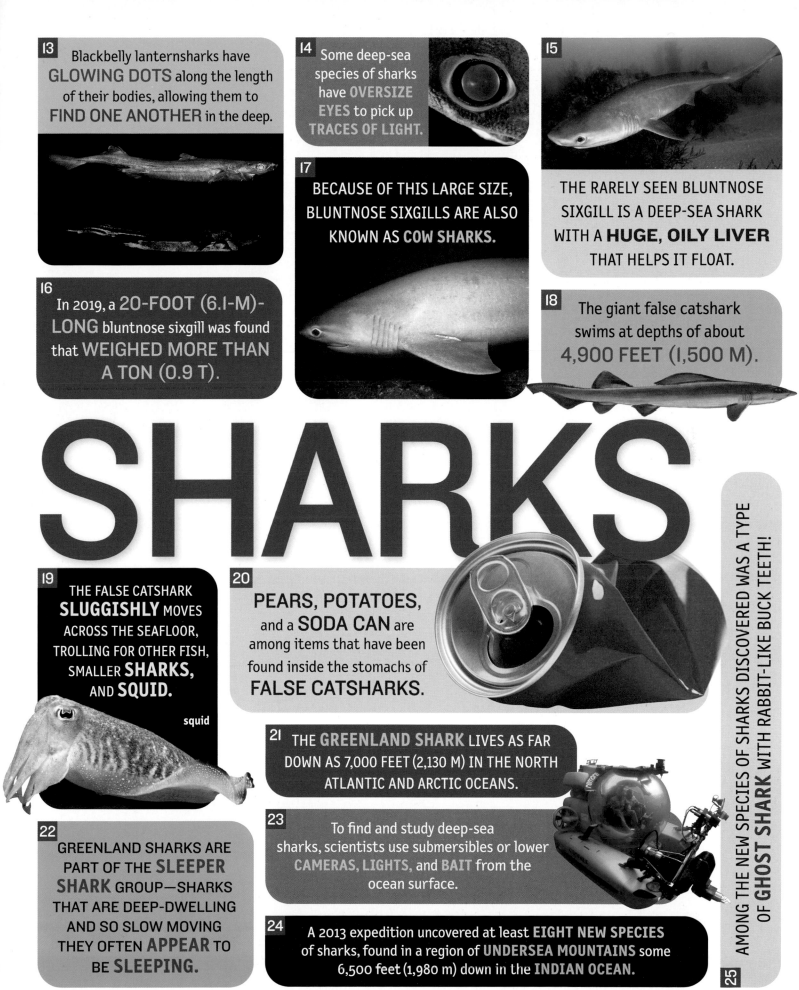

19 THE FALSE CATSHARK **SLUGGISHLY** MOVES ACROSS THE SEAFLOOR, TROLLING FOR OTHER FISH, SMALLER **SHARKS,** AND **SQUID.**

squid

20 PEARS, POTATOES, and a **SODA CAN** are among items that have been found inside the stomachs of **FALSE CATSHARKS.**

21 THE **GREENLAND SHARK** LIVES AS FAR DOWN AS 7,000 FEET (2,130 M) IN THE NORTH ATLANTIC AND ARCTIC OCEANS.

22 GREENLAND SHARKS ARE PART OF THE **SLEEPER SHARK** GROUP—SHARKS THAT ARE DEEP-DWELLING AND SO SLOW MOVING THEY OFTEN **APPEAR** TO BE **SLEEPING.**

23 To find and study deep-sea sharks, scientists use submersibles or lower **CAMERAS, LIGHTS,** and **BAIT** from the ocean surface.

24 A 2013 expedition uncovered at least **EIGHT NEW SPECIES** of sharks, found in a region of **UNDERSEA MOUNTAINS** some 6,500 feet (1,980 m) down in the **INDIAN OCEAN.**

25 AMONG THE NEW SPECIES OF SHARKS DISCOVERED WAS A TYPE OF **GHOST SHARK** WITH RABBIT-LIKE BUCK TEETH!

15 MEGA FACTS ABOUT

❶ The **pygmy shark** can fit easily in the **palm of an adult's hand.**

❷ Little is known about many of the world's smallest sharks, since they live in the **deep sea** and are **rarely seen** by humans.

❸ Even the smallest sharks are **predators,** feasting on **other fish** and **crustaceans.**

❹ These **small swimmers** have rows of tiny, **supersharp teeth.**

❺ It would take **117 dwarf lanternsharks** to be as long as a **whale shark.**

❻ One of the world's smallest sharks, the **dwarf lantern-shark,** is only about the size of a **pencil.**

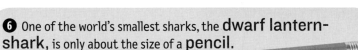

❼ Growing to be just six inches (15 cm) long, the **smalleye pygmy shark** is another pint-size predator in the ocean.

❽ **Green lanternsharks,** which grow to be just 10 inches (25 cm) long, often **attack octopuses** and **squid much larger** than themselves.

THE SMALLEST SHARKS

a coral catshark resting on the seabed off the island of Sulawesi in Indonesia

9 The 160 species of catsharks are fairly small, with most growing to little more than three feet (0.9 m) in length.

10 The spotted-skinned jaguar shark is about the size of a house cat.

11 The 12-inch (30-cm)-long jaguar shark lives in deep water surrounding the Galápagos Islands.

12 Up to 12 tiny babies of the spined pygmy shark develop in a sac that extends from the mother's body.

13 A pygmy ribbontail catshark's pups are about four inches (11 cm) long at birth—already about half the length of their mom.

14 The recently discovered pocket shark—sporting a bulbous head and small fins—is a little bigger than a smartphone.

15 The pocket shark squirts little glowing clouds of pigment in the ocean from tiny pouches near its front fins.

1 Many sharks are **SPECIALLY COLORED** or have a **UNIQUE PATTERN** to blend into their surroundings.

2 A shark's skin color often resembles its **HABITAT**. Nurse sharks, which stick to muddy ocean bottoms, have a **BROWN TOP**.

3 Bottom-dwelling **CAT-SHARKS** are slow swimmers and rely on **BLENDING INTO** the sand with their flat, brownish bodies to stalk prey.

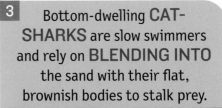

4 The **SALMON SHARK**, found in deeper water, has **DARK GRAY, ALMOST BLACK**, skin, matching its murky surroundings.

5 True to its name, the **BLUE SHARK** has **BRILLIANT BLUE** skin on the top of its body, which helps it blend into the open ocean.

6 Tasselled wobbegongs have a **FLESHY FRINGE** around their heads that looks like **SEAWEED**, helping them blend into the **SEAFLOOR**, where they stalk prey at night.

25 COLORFUL FACTS ABOUT

7 Wobbegongs are also COLORED like MUD and SAND, so they're all but unnoticeable to passing fish and crabs.

8 The wobbegongs' camouflage may also be key in keeping the sharks **HIDDEN** as they **REST** during the day.

9 False **EYESPOTS** on the back of carpet sharks may **TRICK, DISTRACT, OR CONFUSE** their predators.

10 Carpet sharks can also **CHANGE THEIR SKIN COLOR** and **SHADE** to better match the seafloor that surrounds them.

11 This **CHAMELEON EFFECT** is likely due to a shark hormone that causes coloring in the skin to darken and fade.

12 The skin of sharks such as the great white is **countershaded**—it is **dark** on top, **white** underneath, and **silvery** on the sides.

13 Viewed from above, these sharks **BLEND** with the **DARK DEPTHS**. Viewed from below, they blend with the bright **SEA SURFACE**.

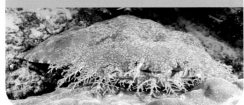

14

Countershading **HELPS** the sharks **HUNT** because prey may not see them until it's **TOO LATE**.

15

WHALES, DOLPHINS, AND PENGUINS ALSO SPORT THIS COLORATION, HELPING THEM AVOID SHARKS.

16

ANGEL SHARKS hide beneath sand on the seabed and wait **PERFECTLY STILL** for their prey.

17

Many **DOGFISH SHARKS** have brown and gray spotted skin, making it hard to spot them near the **SEABED**.

SHARK CAMOUFLAGE

18

With its **GLOWING BELLY**, the golden hammerhead shark blends in with **SUNLIGHT** from **ABOVE**, making it almost **INVISIBLE** from below.

19

Scientists call this trick **COUNTER-ILLUMINATION**, and some squid and several other fish have it as well.

20

A **SWELL SHARK'S** YELLOW SKIN—MARKED BY **BROWN BLOTCHES** AND **WHITE SPOTS**— HELPS IT STAY HIDDEN IN **ROCKY CREVICES**.

25 Zebra sharks also have **RIDGES** along their bodies, mimicking the **TEXTURE OF THE ROCKS** and reefs where they hunt.

21

A young **GOLDEN HAMMERHEAD'S** yellow-orange color helps it blend in with clay-colored silt in the water.

22

A **PYJAMA SHARK'S** striped skin keeps it **CONCEALED** among sea plants as it hides **MOTIONLESS** near its prey, waiting to **STRIKE**.

23

ZEBRA SHARKS are born with spots and **DARK STRIPES** to help camouflage them along the reefs.

24

As they age, zebra sharks' skin becomes more spotted, helping the fish to blend into **SANDY AREAS,** too.

❶ The great white shark lives mostly in cool **coastal waters** in oceans around the world.

❷ The great white gets its name from the **white color** of its **underbelly.**

❸ Its **streamlined shape** and **powerful tail** help propel it through the water at more than 15 miles an hour (24 km/h).

❹ **Young** great whites feed on small prey such as other **fish** and **rays.**

❺ When they're older and bigger, great white sharks seek out **sea turtles** and sea mammals such as **sea lions, seals,** and **small whales.**

❻ While great whites grow to an average of **15 feet (4.6 m)** in length, some have been spotted at more than **20 feet (6.1 m).**

❼ The biggest great whites weigh up to **5,000 pounds (2,270 kg)**—nearly **four times** heavier than a fully grown cow!

close-up of a great white shark

GREAT WHITE SHARK

8 A large adult great white shark is **three times longer** than an adult **person**.

9 The **force** of a great white's **bite** is **four times** stronger than a **tiger's** bite.

10 While in their **mother's womb**, young great whites **swallow their own teeth**, possibly as a source of **calcium**.

11 When hunting seals, great whites **burst out of the water completely**—also known as **breaching**.

12 Unlike most sharks, the great white is **warm-blooded**. It can keep a **high body temperature** even in cold water.

13 Great whites can swim **close to the surface** of the ocean as well as at **depths** of more than 6,000 feet (1,830 m).

14 Dyer Island off the coast of South Africa, often called **Shark Alley**, is home to the world's **biggest population** of great white sharks.

15 A 2019 study shows that great white sharks **fear orcas**, and **swim far away** whenever they cross paths with the killer whales.

1 A group of sharks can be called a **SHIVER, SHOAL, GAM, HERD, FRENZY,** or **SCHOOL.**

2 Sharks tend to live **SEPARATELY** from one another, and typically **SWIM AROUND SOLO.**

4 The main function of shark groups is usually to **hunt down food** in packs—not to create **family bonds.**

3

But not all sharks are **LONERS.** Great white sharks, for example, **KEEP TOGETHER** at mating time.

5 This behavior is known as **COOPERATIVE HUNTING,** and it lets sharks efficiently locate and capture prey.

25 FRENZIED FACTS ABOUT

7 Whitetip reef sharks hunt in groups at **NIGHT** and rest in **CAVES** with other whitetips during the day.

8 Some sharks, like blue sharks, hammerheads, and spiny dogfish, form groups based on **GENDER** and **AGE.**

6

Blacktip reef sharks, thresher sharks, and sand tiger sharks have all been observed **traveling and hunting in packs.**

9 Groups of **YOUNG FEMALE** scalloped hammerheads live offshore in **LARGE SCHOOLS** of up to 500 sharks.

10 Female bonnethead sharks have been spotted **FEASTING** on **BLUE CRABS** together off the shore of South Carolina, U.S.A.

11 Researchers think bonnetheads **COMMUNICATE WITH EACH OTHER** to share the location of certain eating spots.

12 **SCHOOLS OF THOUSANDS** of bonnethead sharks have been spotted swimming in warm, tropical waters.

13 Blacktip reef sharks travel together to find **WARMER WATERS** when the **SEASONS CHANGE.**

14  A group of some 60 to 70 blacktip reef sharks was recently spotted **SWIMMING CLOSE TO THE SHORE** of Peninsula Island in **BALI.**

15 IN 2018, A FRENCH FILMMAKER RECORDED A **FRENZY** OF SOME 700 SHARKS FEEDING ON GROUPER OFF THE COAST OF **POLYNESIA.**

16 During the day, up to 40 nurse sharks **PILE ON TOP OF EACH OTHER** as they rest in caves and rock crevices.

17 LEMON SHARKS **INTERACT** AND **FORM BONDS** WITH ONE ANOTHER IN GROUPS OF 20 TO 40.

SHARK SHIVERS

18 **KEEPING CLOSE** HELPS LEMON SHARKS STAY **SAFE FROM PREDATORS,** LIKE LARGER SHARKS.

19 GREAT WHITE SHARKS TRAVEL IN GROUPS TO **migrate** THROUGH THE OCEANS.

20 Sharks sometimes **HANG OUT PEACEFULLY** with remora fish and other small critters and don't eat them.

21  The sharks and remora fish have a **SYMBIOTIC RELATIONSHIP,** which means they help one another.

22 Remora fish often **HITCH A RIDE** on sharks to **SNACK ON** the sharks' leftover food.

23 In return, the remora remove **DEAD SKIN, MUCUS,** and **PARASITES** from the sharks' skin.

24 Oceanic whitetip sharks **HANG OUT** and hunt with **PODS** of pilot whales.

25 Scientists think these sharks follow the whales to eat their LEFTOVERS—and even **SNACK ON THEIR POOP!**

❶ Rays, skates, and **chimaeras** are related to sharks. They share the same unique dermal denticles, or **placoid scales.**

❷ There are more than **500 different species** of rays and skates. They are divided into **18 families,** or distinct types.

❸ All rays and skates sport a **flattened body,** a skeleton made of **cartilage,** and five or more **gill slits** on each side of the head.

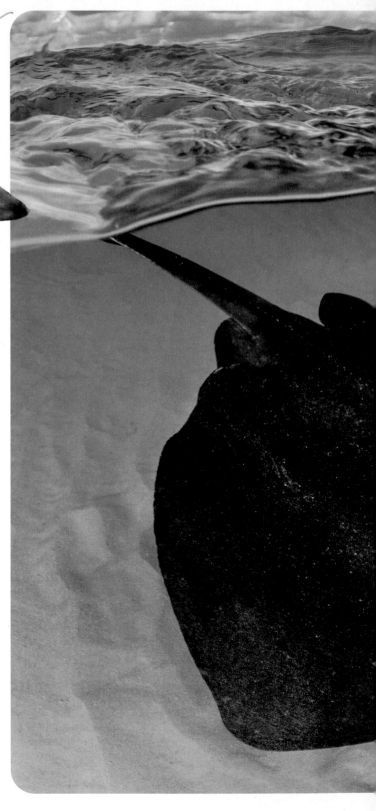

❹ The major difference between rays and skates is **how they have babies:** Rays give birth to live young.

❺ Skates, like many shark species, lay eggs into the water in cases called **mermaid's purses** from which the young emerge.

❻ Skates, compared to rays, also have **large dorsal fins, fleshier tails,** and **thorns on their backs and tails** that are used for protection.

❼ Rays are generally larger than skates, and some have **stinging spines,** or barbs, on their backs and tails.

SHARK COUSINS

8 Not all rays are **stingrays**, however. The **giant manta ray** doesn't have a stinger.

9 **Electric rays,** also known as **torpedo fish** or crampfish, shoot a **strong electric current** from their tails to stun prey.

10 The giant freshwater stingray grows to **16.5 feet (5 m) in length,** including the tail. It **prowls river bottoms** in Thailand, Borneo, New Guinea, and northern Australia.

11 The short-nose electric ray measures just **four inches (10 cm)** across and weighs in at around **one pound (0.5 kg).**

12 Most chimaeras have a venomous spine in front of the dorsal fin and can deliver a **painful jab** with it.

13 They have four gills but only a **single gill opening** on each side of the head, and **smooth skin** without scales. The **largest chimaeras** grow to be about five feet (1.5 m) long.

14 Chimaeras—also known as **ghost sharks** and **spookfish**—are usually found in **deep water** down to 8,500 feet (2,600 m) below the surface.

15 Rays, skates, and chimaeras have been around for a long time. **Fossils** of each have been found dating back more than **150 million years.**

a southern stingray swimming in the Caribbean Sea off the Cayman Islands

1
Sharks' senses of **hearing, touch,** and **smell** are much more powerful than a human's.

2
Sharks use all of their senses when they **hunt and navigate** the **deep,** and often **dark,** oceans.

3
If the **current and light** are just right, a shark can **see movement** up to 50 feet (15.2 m) away.

4
A shark can **feel the flutter** of moving animals in the water **one to two body lengths** away.

5
Sharks' **ears** allow them to hear and to **stay balanced,** just as humans' ears do.

6
Sensory cells in the ears detect **sounds,** and the **shark's speed** and **distance.**

7
Since **sound travels fast** underwater, **hearing** is a key way for sharks to find prey.

8
Sharks can **pick up sounds** below the range of **human hearing.**

9
These **low-frequency sounds** include the noise a **wounded or ill animal** might make.

10
Nerve cells underneath a shark's **snout** provide its **sense of smell.**

11
Some sharks can detect the smell of **one drop of blood** in **25 million drops** of ocean water.

12
That **sensitivity** is enough for a shark to **smell wounded prey** half a mile (0.8 km) away.

13
Because of their superpowered sense of smell, sharks are sometimes called **"swimming noses."**

14
Sharks pick up scents when water flows through their nostrils—or nares—and **triggers nerve cells,** sending signals to the brain.

15
The signals are processed in the **olfactory bulbs—** the parts of the shark's brain that deal with smell.

16
If a shark on the hunt **loses a scent,** it may swim in a wacky S-shaped pattern until it can **pick up the odor** again.

17
By **swinging its head** from side to side, a shark sniffs out the **largest possible area** of water as it swims.

18
Sharks appear to seek out the scent of **amino acids,** which are released in the water by **injured fish and crabs.**

19
Sharks use their **sense of smell** not only for hunting but also to **sniff out potential mates.**

20
Sharks produce **chemicals called pheromones** that attract sharks of the **opposite sex** of the same species.

21
Electroreception— a shark's **"sixth sense"**—is the ability to pick up electrical signals from other living creatures.

22
All living things produce an **electronic field,** created by the chemical activity of their cells.

23
Sharks use these **faint electrical charges** to sense the **flow of water.**

24
A shark's **snout and body** are covered in thousands of **tiny gel-filled pores.**

25
These **unique organs,** called ampullae, can detect **faint electrical signals** given off by fish.

26
Each ampulla contains **sensory cells** and **nerves** connected to the shark's brain.

27
Using electroreception, sharks can find prey even if they're **hidden in the sand.**

28
Other animals, like the platypus and bumblebee, have **electroreception,** but a shark's is **the most sensitive.**

29
Sharks can also sense electrical fields from **boats** and other **objects** used by people in the water.

30
Sharks build an **electrical "map"** of their surroundings, allowing them to **find prey and avoid predators.**

31
This map also helps them travel long distances **without losing their way.**

32
Scientists think that certain sharks, like hammerheads, can tune into **Earth's magnetic field.**

33
This would explain how some sharks can **swim in straight lines** for long periods of time.

34
Every shark has a **lateral line**—a tube filled with fluid—running down **each side of its body.**

35
The **tubes** are open to the surrounding water through **tiny pores.**

36
The lateral lines allow a shark to sense **pressure waves** produced by **movements or sounds** in the water around it.

37
The lines also **detect large nearby objects,** since water changes direction when it flows around them.

38
Sharks can sense changes in **temperature** of the water around them.

39
A shark's senses help it detect when a **major storm,** like a hurricane, is coming.

40
The lateral line system can detect **sudden drops in pressure in the atmosphere,** which hurricanes cause.

41
Sharks' eyes are sensitive to **light, movement,** and **color.**

42
Their eyes have a layer of **mirrored crystals** behind the retina called the **tapetum lucidum.**

43
The crystals **reflect light** and allow sharks to see very well at night and in dark waters.

44
In the dark, a shark's eyes are **10 times more sensitive to light** than a human's eyes.

45
A **puffadder shyshark's eyes** are so sensitive to light that it will curl its tail back to **cover its eyes** if it's pulled out of the water.

46
The **bigeye thresher** has enormous eyes that help it see well in **low light.**

47
Taste—detected by buds, or groups of sensory cells inside its mouth—is the **least developed** of a shark's senses.

48
The **taste buds** help a shark **identify food** before it eats it.

49
Sharks can be **picky** and will spit out food that **tastes unpleasant** to them.

50
Nurse sharks and saw sharks have **sensitive barbels** drooping from the mouth that can feel for prey in murky water.

nurse sharks on the hunt for food

50 SUPERPOWERED FACTS ABOUT SHARK SENSES

1 At up to 32 FEET (9.8 M) long, the BASKING SHARK is the second largest fish in the ocean, after the whale shark.

2 The shark got its name from how it lies on its back on the water's surface LIKE A SUNBATHER.

3 THE BASKING SHARK INHABITS ALL OCEANS OF THE WORLD.

4 THE SHARK SPENDS ABOUT 90 PERCENT OF ITS TIME DEEP UNDER-WATER, AND ONLY 10 PERCENT AT THE SURFACE.

5 It is usually found at depths of between 650 AND 3,300 FEET (200 AND 1,000 M).

25 UNFILTERED FACTS ABOUT

6 THE BASKING SHARK IS ONE OF THREE PLANKTON-EATING SHARKS, ALONG WITH WHALE SHARKS AND MEGAMOUTH SHARKS.

7 It is **NOT AGGRESSIVE** and is **HARMLESS TO HUMANS.**

8 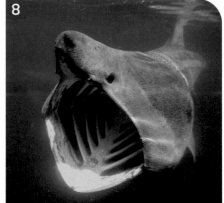 THE BASKING SHARK HAS HUNDREDS OF **tiny teeth,** BUT IT DOESN'T USE THEM TO EAT OR HUNT.

9 Instead, it opens its mouth wide to **SUCK IN GALLONS OF WATER,** then strains the water out through its gills to **TRAP THE PLANKTON INSIDE.**

10 An adult basking shark's MOUTH is about as wide as a TWO-YEAR-OLD HUMAN IS TALL.

11

12 Some 1,400 **BASKING SHARKS** once gathered off the coast of southern New England, U.S.A., likely **FEEDING ON ZOOPLANKTON.**

 SCIENTISTS RECENTLY FOUND A BASKING SHARK CAN STRAIN AT LEAST 1,800 TONS (1,630 T) OF WATER THROUGH ITS GILLS IN ONE HOUR.

13 Despite being a SLOW SWIMMER—it rarely breaks THREE MILES AN HOUR (5 KM/H)—a basking shark can jump entirely out of the water.

14 It may make these leaps, or BREACH, to rid its skin of EELS AND OTHER PARASITES.

15 In 2008, waves created by a breaching basking shark CAPSIZED A SMALL BOAT off the coast of Scotland.

16 The basking shark produces a mucus-based slime that covers its skin, likely to fight off parasites.

17 The slime is CORROSIVE enough to burn through the natural fibers of fishing nets and is said to be SUPER STINKY.

18 A YOUNG BASKING SHARK HAS A LONG, HOOK-SHAPED SNOUT. AS THE SHARK GROWS, ITS SNOUT STRAIGHTENS OUT.

THE BASKING SHARK

19 A basking shark's OIL-FILLED LIVER makes up 25 percent of its body weight.

20 In the 1700s and 1800s, basking shark liver oil was used as LAMP FUEL.

21 CHEMICALS IN THE OIL HAVE ALSO BEEN USED IN MEDICINE AND AS INGREDIENTS IN PERFUMES.

22 AS A RESULT, THE BASKING SHARK WAS HEAVILY HUNTED BY PEOPLE FROM THE 1700s TO THE 1990s.

23 At one point, the basking shark was considered NEARLY EXTINCT.

24 Today, the basking shark is considered a VULNERABLE SPECIES, which means it faces the threat of BECOMING ENDANGERED if its numbers decline.

25 It's now ILLEGAL TO HUNT the basking shark in many places around the world.

Just Arrived in the Metropolis! And to be seen in a Spacious Yard, In North Audley Street. GROSVENOR SQUARE, A Most Stupendous BASKING SHARK! Caught within One League of BRIGHTON, On SATURDAY last, the 5th Inst. AND PURCHASED FOR £600. Measuring in Length upwards of 30 Feet, in Circumference 18 Feet, and Weighing EIGHT TONS. This Astonishing Sea Monster!!!

75 LIVELY FACTS ABOUT SHARK LIFE CYCLES

1 All sharks are born from eggs, but the eggs develop in one of two main ways.

2 In some shark species, the eggs grow into babies inside the mom and babies are born live.

3 IN ALL OTHER SHARK SPECIES, THE EGGS ARE RELEASED INTO THE WATER IN TOUGH, PROTECTIVE CASES, AND THE BABIES HATCH FROM THESE.

4 About 70 percent of sharks, including hammerhead, bull, and blue sharks, are viviparous, giving birth to live young.

5 Developing young viviparous sharks get nourishment within their mom's womb from a placenta and umbilical cord, like mammals.

6 Sharks that lay eggs into the water are oviparous, like birds.

7 If a shark has eggs that hatch inside the mother's body, and then the babies are born live, it is called ovoviviparous.

8 Oviparous sharks are mostly bottom-feeders, and include horn sharks and catsharks.

9 AN OVIPAROUS SHARK'S EGG CASES ARE CALLED MERMAID'S PURSES.

10 Mermaid's purses are made from keratin, the same material that makes up human hair and fingernails.

11 Mermaid's purses are camouflaged to blend in with the seafloor or algae.

an egg case of a catshark attached to coral in the Mediterranean Sea

12 Each egg case usually houses one embryo, but in some species there are multiple baby sharks inside.

13 THE EGG CASES HAVE TENDRILS THAT ALLOW THEM TO ATTACH TO CORAL OR SEAWEED SO THEY STAY HIDDEN FROM POTENTIAL PREDATORS.

14 Shark eggs are vulnerable to attack from fish, marine mammals, and even large mollusks.

15 Egg-laying shark moms take time to look for good hiding places for their eggs.

16 Horn sharks hide their egg cases in cracks between rocks or bury them in the sandy ocean bottom.

17 Port Jackson shark eggs are each encased in a rock-hard, spiral-shaped mermaid's purse.

18 When the shark babies, called pups, are ready to be born, their egg case splits open and they wiggle out.

19 As a baby shark in an egg case hatches, it uses its tail to pump fresh seawater into the case so it can breathe.

20 It may take one month or up to a year before a shark is ready to hatch, depending on the species.

21 OF THE SHARKS THAT GIVE BIRTH TO LIVE YOUNG, MOST SPECIES ARE OVOVIVIPAROUS.

22 Cookiecutters, the great white, and sand tigers are all examples of ovoviviparous sharks.

23 After they hatch, the larger pups of sand tiger sharks kill and eat the smaller pups while still inside their mom's womb.

24 This process is known as embryophagy.

25 The pups of ovoviviparous thresher, mako, and salmon sharks feed on their mother's eggs while in the womb.

26 This is known as oophagy, which means "egg eating."

27 The young of egg-eating sharks are often born with a swollen belly that experts call a yolk stomach.

28 Ovoviviparous shark moms nourish their pups growing inside them with nutrient-rich milk before they're born.

29 SOME RAYS ARE OVOVIVIPAROUS. THE REST ARE OVIPAROUS, AS ARE ALL CHIMAERAS.

30 Females of big shark species are pregnant for longer than those of smaller species.

31 Shark species that live in both cold and deep waters tend to have longer pregnancies because their metabolism— or body chemistry—works at a slow pace.

32 A mother lemon shark gives birth in a "nursery"—a safe, warm, and shallow spot with plenty of shelter and food for her pups.

33 Species such as the spiny dogfish and basking shark carry their babies for more than two years before delivery.

34 All shark pups come into the world as fully formed predators. They start feeding right away.

35 Before they're born, shark pups start losing and replacing teeth—as they will in adult life.

36 A hammerhead shark is born with its head bent backward so it doesn't get stuck during delivery.

37 Some species of sharks usually have just two offspring at a time, while others have many more.

38 A blue shark mother can give birth to more than 80 babies at one time.

39 Once, a female blue shark gave birth to 135 pups in a single litter!

40 Great white shark moms usually have anywhere between two and 10 pups.

41 One great white shark had a record-setting litter of 15 pups.

42 Gray nurse sharks have the lowest reproductive rate known for sharks, producing about two pups every two years.

43 Tiger sharks have one of the highest reproductive rates among sharks, giving birth to an average of 30 pups every three years.

44 WHEN A SHARK GIVES BIRTH, IT'S ALSO KNOWN AS PUPPING.

45 Throughout the spring and summer, female California horn sharks lay about two eggs every two weeks.

46 Although rare, some sharks can reproduce via asexual reproduction, known as parthenogenesis.

47 This means the female sharks don't need a male mate to have babies.

48 Hammerhead sharks and zebra sharks living in captivity have produced young in this manner.

49 Pups born through parthenogenesis are genetically identical to their mothers.

50 Baby sharks start to look like mini versions of adults very early on in development.

51 Scientists observed a tawny nurse shark swimming at a rate of three inches (7.6 cm) per second while inside its mother's womb.

52 While still in their egg cases, baby brownbanded bamboosharks can sense the electric fields of predators.

53 If a predator is nearby, these tiny unborn sharks will freeze in place to avoid detection.

54 Shark parents do not take care of their young. As soon as the pups hatch or are born into the water, they swim away and care for themselves.

55 Shark siblings don't stick together. Once a shark is born or hatches, it's on its own.

56 Shark pups are often preyed upon by larger sharks, bigger fish, and birds.

57 IN THE WILD, FEMALE SHARKS START TO HAVE BABIES WHEN THEY'RE AROUND 10 YEARS OLD, DEPENDING ON THE SPECIES.

58 Female great white sharks don't typically reproduce until they're around 12 to 18 years old.

59 In some cases, it may take 33 years before a female great white shark is ready to have babies.

60 For some species of sharks, it's possible to tell how old they are by looking at growth layers on their spine and fins.

61 Counting these hardened layers, or growth bands, is similar to counting rings on a tree trunk.

62 Scientists also test for traces of radioactivity in growth bands, an even more accurate way to age a shark.

63 If a shark tests positive for radioactivity, it was likely alive during nuclear bomb testing of the 1950s and 1960s, which left radiocarbon in the ocean.

64 Researchers also look at small pieces of tissue in the center of a shark's eye lens to determine its age.

65 The eye lens grows throughout a shark's life, adding layers like an onion's.

66 USING THIS METHOD, RESEARCHERS AGED ONE GREENLAND SHARK TO BE MORE THAN 400 YEARS OLD.

67 The spiny dogfish and whale shark are known to live 100 years or longer.

68 The blue shark has an average life expectancy of about 15 years.

69 Sharks do not live as long in captivity, perhaps due to a lack of activity.

70 One tiger shark named Bertha lived in a tank at the New York Aquarium until she was about 43.

71 Before she died, Bertha was one of the oldest sharks in any aquarium in the world.

72 In the wild, sharks typically die of natural causes, like organ failure.

73 Some species are killed by other sharks or predators like elephant seals and orcas.

74 Scientists say some sharks can develop cancer.

75 When a shark dies, the salty ocean water completely dissolves its skeleton, leaving only its teeth behind.

1
There are more than **30 SPECIES** of **CARPET SHARK.**

2
All carpet sharks have **broad, flat heads** with mouths in front of **small eyes.**

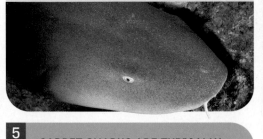

3
Carpet sharks also have **FLATTENED BODIES,** two dorsal fins, five pairs of gill slits, and **PIGLIKE SNOUTS.**

4
Many carpet sharks have **BARBELS** that hang off their snouts.

5
CARPET SHARKS ARE TYPICALLY FOUND IN **WARM, SHALLOW WATERS** OF THE ATLANTIC, PACIFIC, AND INDIAN OCEANS.

6
MANY LIVE ON THE SEABED—LIKE RUGS OR CARPETS ON THE OCEAN FLOOR.

25 COOL FACTS ABOUT

8

MOST CARPET SHARKS ARE **BOTTOM-FEEDERS,** WITH A DIET OF **MOLLUSKS** AND **CRUSTACEANS.**

9
NURSE SHARKS, a type of carpet shark, are referred to as the **COUCH POTATOES** of the shark world.

7
Carpet sharks are **NOT CONSIDERED DANGEROUS** to humans, but they may **PROTECT THEMSELVES** if threatened.

10
THESE **slow-moving bottom-dwellers** SPEND THEIR DAYS IN WARM SHALLOW SEAS.

11
Some carpet sharks are fierce hunters: In 2012, a **WOBBEGONG**—a type of carpet shark—was seen **SWALLOWING A BAMBOOSHARK WHOLE.**

12
The wobbegong's **NAME** is from the native Australian word for **"SHAGGY BEARD."**

13
WOBBEGONGS HAVE **SUPERSHARP TEETH** THAT ALLOW THEM TO RELENTLESSLY CLAMP DOWN ON PREY.

14 WOBBEGONG SHARKS CAN **open their mouths wide enough** TO SWALLOW PREY **their own size.**

15 The speckled carpet shark will eat only BITE-SIZE PIECES OF FOOD.

16 THE LARGEST CARPET SHARK IS THE **WHALE SHARK—** THE BIGGEST FISH OF ALL.

17 The smallest carpet shark of all is THE BARBELTHROAT CARPET SHARK, which measures about 12 INCHES (30 CM) LONG.

CARPET SHARKS

18 THE WHALE SHARK IS THE ONLY FILTER-FEEDING CARPET SHARK.

19 The **BLIND SHARK,** a type of carpet shark, isn't actually blind: It just keeps its **EYES SHUT** when it's out of the water.

20 THE BLIND SHARK IS **NOCTURNAL,** FEEDING AT NIGHT AND HIDING IN HOLES DURING THE DAY.

21 The **NECKLACE CARPET SHARK** is named for its telltale dark collar with white spots, like a **STRING OF PEARLS.**

22 Found on MUDDY, SANDY, OR ROCKY BOTTOMS, collared carpet sharks can CHANGE COLOR to match the seafloor.

25 CARPET SHARKS CAN **PUMP WATER** OVER THEIR GILLS TO BREATHE EVEN WHILE THEY'RE RESTING AT THE BOTTOM OF THE SEA.

23 LIKE NURSE SHARKS, **BAMBOO-SHARKS** USE THEIR MUSCULAR PECTORAL FINS TO **CRAWL ON THE SEAFLOOR.**

24 The bambooshark is also known as the LONGTAIL CARPET SHARK, because its tail is often LONGER THAN ITS BODY.

❶ *Sphyrna*, the **genus name** of most hammerhead sharks, comes from the **Greek word for** "hammer."

❷ In biology, the **hammerhead shape** of this shark's noggin is called a **cephalofoil.**

❸ There are **10 species** of hammerhead sharks, ranging from nearly five feet (1.5 m) to **20 feet (6.1 m)** in length.

❹ A hammerhead's **wide-set eyes** probably give it extremely good binocular vision.

❺ The mouth of the hammerhead, used to snatch food, is **fairly small.**

❻ Hammerheads seek out **catfish, small bony fish, lobsters,** and their favorite snack— **stingrays.**

❼ Scoophead, bonnethead, and scalloped bonnethead sharks are all types of hammerheads, but have **rounder heads** that look more like the end of a shovel.

❽ Young **scalloped hammerheads** can get a **suntan** when swimming in shallow water.

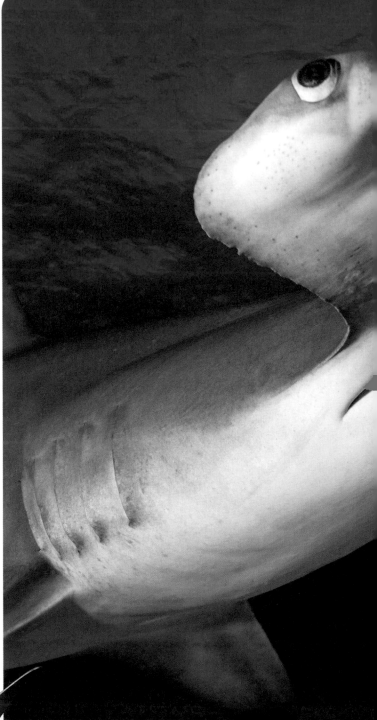

a great hammerhead shark, the largest species of the hammerhead shark family

HAMMERHEAD SHARKS

9 The hammerhead has a **special neck muscle** that allows it to swiftly move its head **up and down.**

10 While swimming, hammerheads will **roll over and swim sideways** to save energy.

11 Relative to its body size, the **winghead shark** has the **widest head** of any hammerhead—almost as wide as half its body length.

12 A hammerhead's body is **specially designed to twist and bend,** allowing the fish to make very **sudden and sharp turns.**

13 Hammerhead sharks are **wary** and generally **avoid people.**

14 According to scientists' **DNA studies,** the common ancestor of the hammerheads probably lived about **20 million years ago.**

15 When food is scarce, a hungry hammerhead mom may **eat her young** after they are born.

⑮ COMMEMORATIVE

❶ The Whale Shark Festival takes place every July in Isla Mujeres, Mexico. People celebrate the giant fish, which gather to feed there in the thousands.

the infamous park bench in Bangkok

❷ The San Jose Sharks professional hockey team's name was inspired by the many sharks living in the Pacific Ocean off the coast of California, U.S.A.

❸ Part of the 20,702-foot (6,310-m) Meru Peak in India, Shark Fin's route—named for its finlike shape—is known as one of the most difficult climbs in the world.

GREAT WHITE SHARK

❹ In 2017, the U.S. Postal Service sold exclusive Sharks Forever stamps, featuring the great white, hammerhead, mako, thresher, and whale sharks.

❺ Venice, Florida, U.S.A., is considered the Sharks Tooth Capital of the World because of the millions of shark teeth that wash up on its beaches.

❻ Every April, Venice hosts its Sharks Tooth Festival, highlighting fossil collectors who display and sell sharks' teeth.

❼ A blue shark was featured on a 2008 $1 coin used on the Pacific Island of Palau.

❽ A giant great white shark statue sits behind a riverside park bench in Bangkok, Thailand. The larger-than-life shark appears to be leaping out of the ground, ready to chomp on anyone who sits on the bench.

FACTS ABOUT SHARKS

9 For a **$50 donation,** you can name a shark **tagged by the University of Miami Shark Research center** in Florida, and receive updates and data they collect on the fish.

10 There's a 25-foot (7.6-m)-long fiberglass **shark sculpture crashing headfirst** into the roof of a house in Headington, Oxford, in the United Kingdom.

11 Despite its name, Shark's Cove snorkeling site in Oahu, Hawai'i, U.S.A., isn't a hot spot for sharks. It's actually named for the outline of the underwater reefs that resemble a shark's head.

12 The **Costa Rican 2,000 colones banknote** depicts a bull shark swimming around a coral reef. The predator is native to waters around the country's **Bat Island.**

13 Some aquariums and conservation groups celebrate Sharktober each October— a chance to raise awareness of and celebrate sharks with film fests, parties, and other activities.

14 Surabaya, a city name in Indonesia that means "courage to face danger," is represented by many statues, each showing a shark fighting a crocodile.

15 Shark Awareness Day—July 14—is a way to increase info about sharks and their importance in marine ecosystems.

1 Because they're such **EFFICIENT SWIMMERS** and have been around for **MILLIONS OF YEARS,** sharks are often studied to **CREATE NEW INVENTIONS.**

2 **GETTING INSPIRATION FROM ANIMALS** like sharks to create new technology is a field of science known as **BIOMIMICRY.**

3 A **WATER TURBINE** in the shape of a shark's tail has been created to **HARNESS WAVE ENERGY** and convert it into electricity.

4 The design for the **MAKO SHARK CORVETTE** was hatched after the car's designer caught a mako on a **FISHING TRIP.**

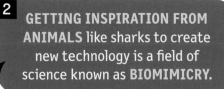

5 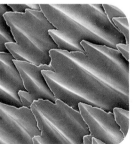 The look of the BMW ALPHA **LANDSPEEDER MOTORCYCLE** was inspired by the body shape of the great white shark.

25 HIGH-TECH FACTS ABOUT SHARK-INSPIRED

6 **3D-PRINTED SHARK SKIN** allows water to flow over it **6 PERCENT FASTER** than over a smooth plastic surface.

7 The skin of a **shortfin mako** has been scanned to design a **3D-printed aerofoil,** the part of a plane's wing that helps it lift off and stay controlled.

8 THE MAKO-BASED AEROFOIL MAY ONE DAY BE USED IN **DRONES** AND **AIRPLANES.**

9 At the **2004 OLYMPIC GAMES** in Athens, Greece, some **SWIMMERS WORE SUITS** made of a material based on shark skin.

10 Designed to **REDUCE DRAG** in the water, the "Fastskin" suits featured V-shaped ridges, like a shark's **DERMAL DENTICLES** (also known as placoid scales).

11 **FASTSKIN SUITS,** thought to reduce drag for swimmers, didn't help people swim like sharks—but they did help swimmers go faster, and were soon **BANNED** from all swimming competitions for giving athletes an unfair advantage.

12 *Seabreacher X,* AN UNDERWATER SUBMERSIBLE, IS SHAPED LIKE A SHARK AND CAN LAUNCH OUT OF THE WATER TO *mimic breaching.*

13 THE **GHOSTSWIMMER,** AN UNDERWATER DRONE THAT CAN DIVE DOWN TO 300 FEET (91 M), **LOOKS AND SWIMS LIKE A REAL SHARK.**

14 Scientists are using synthetic shark skin to create **AQUATIC ROBOTS FOR UNDERWATER EXPLORATION.**

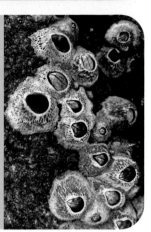

15 **EXTRACTS FROM SHARK CARTILAGE** seem to combat **CANCER CELLS** and boost the **IMMUNE SYSTEM** of humans.

17 Shark skin is **RESISTANT TO ALGAE AND BARNACLES,** inspiring scientists to create a coating for **SHIPS' HULLS** that prevents bacteria from attaching.

16 Shark cartilage has been used in OINTMENTS TO TREAT SEVERE BURNS.

SCIENCE AND TECHNOLOGY

18 The same coating—called Sharklet—is used in **HOSPITALS** to prevent harmful bacteria from **STICKING TO WORK SURFACES.**

19 Using **lasers,** the intricate structure of shark skin has been created to make a **supersleek metal.**

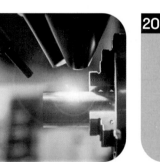

20 The metal may be used to create **SUBMERSIBLES** that can travel **FARTHER UNDERWATER USING LESS POWER.**

21 Scientists are experimenting with the gel found in some sharks' electro-sensory ampullae that can convert heat energy into electricity.

22 A SYNTHETIC FORM OF THE GEL is being tested to transform HEAT FROM A CAR ENGINE into usable electricity.

25 ROTTEN SHARK TISSUE is the key ingredient in some **SPRAYS AND WAXES** used by swimmers and surfers to repel sharks.

23 FOR A FEW HUNDRED DOLLARS, YOU CAN BUY A **GADGET THAT REPELS SHARKS** BY SAFELY INTERFERING WITH THEIR SENSITIVITY TO ELECTRICAL FIELDS.

24 THE DEVICE EMITS AN **ELECTRICAL CURRENT THAT** overstimulates **A SHARK'S SENSORY ORGANS,** prompting the fish to swim away **FROM A POTENTIAL VICTIM.**

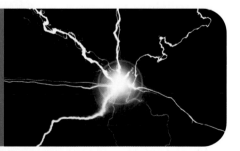

1 The BIGGEST SHARK OF ALL TIME? *Carcharodon megalodon*, which ruled the waters about 5 MILLION YEARS AGO.

2 Megalodon is estimated to have grown to 60 FEET (18 M) LONG and up to 27.6 TONS (25 T) IN WEIGHT.

3 A FULL-GROWN MEGALODON was about the same size and weight as a FULLY LOADED SEMITRUCK.

4 Megalodon's MOUTH was so big, an adult human could have easily CLIMBED INSIDE IT.

5 Megalodon means "BIG TOOTH" in Greek, and these sharks certainly had huge chompers—as long as eight inches (20 cm).

6 A NEWBORN WHALE SHARK in captivity went from 1.7 pounds to 333.4 pounds (0.8 to 151 kg) IN JUST THREE YEARS.

7 The heaviest whale shark in captivity WEIGHED SEVEN TONS (6.4 T)—the weight of a LARGE AFRICAN ELEPHANT.

8 Prior to hatching inside their mother's womb, WHALE SHARK EGGS are about as BIG AS A FOOTBALL.

9 Whale sharks have a huge mouth but a TINY THROAT, measuring just about the SIZE OF A U.S. QUARTER.

10 BOTTOM-DWELLING GOBLIN SHARKS are among the biggest swimmers in the seas, growing as long as 13 feet (4 m).

11 An ADULT GOBLIN SHARK can weigh more than 400 pounds (181 kg).

a whale shark

35 MASSIVE FACTS ABOUT

12 A young girl found a fossilized MEGALODON TOOTH as big as her hand in the sand at Topsail Beach, North Carolina, U.S.A.

13 A full-grown WHALE SHARK is about THREE-FIFTHS the size of megalodon.

14 As big as a football stadium, the WHALE SHARK TANK at the GEORGIA AQUARIUM in Atlanta, U.S.A., is the world's largest.

15 The aquarium is the only one in the WESTERN HEMISPHERE to house these MASSIVE SHARKS.

16 At the huge OKINAWA AQUARIUM in Japan, whale sharks swim around in a FOUR-STORY-TALL TANK.

17 In Pakistan in 2012, it took FIVE CRANES to lift a 40-foot (12-m) dead WHALE SHARK out of the water to be examined.

18 BIG SHARK SPECIES are fairly RARE. Most shark species are less than three feet (1 m) long.

19 The GREENLAND SHARK, which lives in cold, dark Arctic waters, grows AS LONG AS 24 FEET (7.3 M).

20 Relative to its LARGE SIZE, the Greenland shark has VERY SMALL FINS.

21 A large PACIFIC SLEEPER SHARK was mistaken for a MEGALODON in a 2016 VIRAL VIDEO.

22 In 1945, FISHERS IN CUBA once reeled in a 21-FOOT (6.4-M), 7,000-POUND (3,175-KG) great white shark.

23 Scientific evidence shows that the great white may have EVOLVED from the MEGALODON LINE of sharks.

24 A 20-foot (6.1-m)-long female great white named DEEP BLUE is one of the BIGGEST of its species CAUGHT ON FILM.

25 Researchers have been TRACKING Deep Blue for years, and she's been seen off the coasts of MEXICO and HAWAI'I, U.S.A.

26 In 2019, a young 9-foot (2.7-m)-long BASKING SHARK was spotted off the coast of DEVON, U.K., a record size for U.K. waters.

27 The basking shark can reach 33 feet (10 m) long—big enough TO SWALLOW A PERSON WHOLE—but is only a filter feeder.

28 A BLUE SHARK PUP will grow about 12 INCHES (30 CM) EACH YEAR until it reaches maturity at five years old.

29 Most sharks grow less than A QUARTER OF AN INCH (6 MM) IN A YEAR, taking decades to reach full size.

30 A female cow shark is actually MUCH LARGER THAN A COW, reaching a maximum length of more than 15 FEET (4.6 M).

31 Given their size and hunting skills, great white, bull, and tiger sharks are considered the BIG THREE shark attack species.

32 In 2019, a family boating off CAPE COD, U.S.A., was visited by a GREAT WHITE shark 16 feet (4.9 m) long.

33 A 14.5-foot (4.4-m)-long HAMMERHEAD shark was spotted SWALLOWING a BLACKTIP SHARK off the coast of Florida, U.S.A.

34 In 2019, golfer GREG NORMAN, whose golf nickname is "The Shark," caught a record-size hammerhead.

35 In 2020, a great white 15 feet 5 inches (4.6 m) long was tracked in the ocean from NOVA SCOTIA, Canada, to LOUISIANA, U.S.A.

SUPERSIZE SHARKS

15 FIERCE FACTS ABOUT THE

1 The bull shark gets its name from its **short snout**, plus the way it **head-butts its prey** before attacking.

2 Female bull sharks typically measure five feet (1.5 m) longer than males.

3 A bull shark has a **barrel-shaped body** that is **much wider** compared to its length than other sharks' bodies are.

4 The bull shark lives in **warm waters**, preferring shallow spots in the **Atlantic Ocean** along the coasts of the U.S., South America, and Africa, as well as the **Indian Ocean** along the coast of Africa.

5 While the majority of sharks can live **only in salt water**, the bull shark has the special ability to swim in **both salt water and fresh water.**

6 Scientists think the bull shark can swim in fresh water for long periods of time because its **kidneys** and a **special gland near its tail** help it **store unwanted salt** in its body.

7 One bull shark was found swimming in the **Amazon River** about 2,500 miles (4,020 km) away from the ocean. Another was spotted swimming as far as 1,500 miles (2,410 km) up the **Mississippi River**.

8 Bull sharks have been spotted **leaping over river rapids.**

a bull shark swimming off the coast of Cuba

BULL SHARK

9 Because they're so **aggressive**—and because they tend to hunt where **people swim**—experts consider the bull shark one of the **most dangerous species of sharks.**

10 Bull sharks are known to **bump then bite other animals** out of **curiosity,** not because they're hungry.

11 The bull shark's typical diet consists of **oysters, turtles, and other fish—including sharks**—but it is also known to go after much bigger prey, such as **hippos** basking in shallow waters.

12 Although rare, bull sharks have been recorded eating other bull sharks.

13 Young bull sharks have a **black tip on their fins,** which fades as the fish grow.

14 **Golfers** at a course in Brisbane, Australia, putt around a lake that's **home to bull sharks.** The sharks arrived when a nearby river flooded the course, and they stayed in the lake when the water receded.

15 The Oklahoma Aquarium in Tulsa, Oklahoma, U.S.A., has the largest collection of bull sharks in captivity in the world—a group of 10.

1 Almost all species of sharks are naturally built for **SUDDEN BURSTS OF SPEED.**

2 Sharks **RELY HEAVILY** on their speed in the water to **ATTACK PREY.**

3 The fastest sharks—the **SHORTFIN MAKO, SALMON,** and **GREAT WHITE**—are all types of **MACKEREL SHARK.**

4 THE **SHORTFIN MAKO SHARK** CAN SWIM IN SPEEDY BURSTS, POSSIBLY REACHING SPEEDS OF OVER **45 miles an hour (72 km/h).**

5 A shortfin mako can zip across the length of an **Olympic swimming pool** in about **two seconds.**

25 SPEEDY FACTS ABOUT THE

6 The average shark **SWIMS AROUND** at speeds of about **1.5 MILES AN HOUR (2.4 KM/H).**

7 A young shortfin mako has been recorded accelerating from a dead stop **FASTER THAN A PORSCHE SPORTS CAR!**

8 A **SHORTFIN MAKO CAN** OFTEN **OUTSWIM** POTENTIAL PREDATORS, LIKE ADULT ORCAS.

9 Still, the shortfin mako is **NOT THE FASTEST FISH** in the ocean: That's the **SAILFISH,** which can top speeds of 70 miles an hour (113 km/h).

10 A MAKO'S **SECRET TO SPEED?** SCIENTISTS SAY IT'S THE **EXTRA-FLEXIBLE DERMAL DENTICLES** ON ITS SKIN, WHICH REDUCE DRAG.

11 The shortfin mako's **TORPEDO-SHAPED BODY** helps it **CUT THROUGH** the water.

12 A shortfin mako's speed gives it the ability to **LEAP OUT OF THE WATER.**

13

A LEAPING MAKO SHARK **SHOOTS OUT OF WATER** AT A SPEED OF ABOUT **36 MILES AN HOUR (58 KM/H)**. IT CRASHES BACK WITH A BIG SPLASH.

14 A shortfin mako's close cousin, the **LONGFIN MAKO**, is believed to be **SLOWER AND LESS ACTIVE** than its relative.

15 The **SALMON SHARK** has been observed swimming as fast as **50 MILES AN HOUR (80.5 KM/H)**.

16 Like the mako, the salmon shark has a **MUSCULAR, STREAMLINED BODY.**

17

The **SALMON SHARK** is warm-blooded, which allows its muscles to work more efficiently so it **CAN SWIM FASTER** than its prey in cold environments.

FASTEST SHARKS

18 A powerful **CAUDAL FIN**— or tail fin—allows the salmon shark to speed forward while exerting minimum **ENERGY.**

19 A **GREAT WHITE SHARK** can swim at 25 miles an hour (40.2 km/h)—five times faster than a human's speed in a pool.

20 Olympic **GOLD MEDAL** swimmer Michael Phelps once "raced" a great white shark—or rather a **COMPUTER-GENERATED IMAGE OF ONE.**

21 The result of the race? Phelps, wearing a **special wet suit and fin,** swam 100 meters in **38.1 seconds.** The shark's time? **36.1 seconds.**

22 Despite its barrel-shaped body, the **BULL SHARK** can reach speeds of up to 24 miles an hour (39 km/h) when **CHASING PREY.**

23 The **tiger shark** and the **blue shark** can each top 20 miles an hour (32 km/h) when **hunting** in calm waters.

24

The fastest sharks **PICK UP SPEED** by **STIFFENING** their **TAIL** and using it like a **POWERFUL** rudder to steer.

25 A great white shark may be speedy when **STALKING PREY,** but it **SLOWS DOWN** dramatically when **READY TO POUNCE** on a victim.

15 MYTHICAL FACTS ABOUT

1 Although the term "sharke" was first used in the English language in 1569, stories of the fish group date back to **ancient times.**

2 **Lamnidae sharks**—a family that includes the great white shark—are named after **Lamia,** a woman who turns into a shark in one **ancient Greek myth.**

3 In medieval Europe, Saint Nicholas, **protector of seafarers,** was believed to save shipwrecked sailors from **sea creatures** such as sharks.

4 **Ancient Hawaiians** worshipped several **shark gods, including Kauhuhu,** who was said to **live in a cave** on the side of a cliff protected by dragons.

5 They also honored the shark goddess Ka'ahupahau, said to live at the entrance of **Pearl Harbor,** who **drove off man-eating sharks.**

6 One Indigenous Australian tribe believes a **mythical giant tiger shark** had caused a real-life rock formation to turn red with blood after a particularly **fierce sea battle.**

7 **Goblin sharks** were first named by **Japanese fishers** for their likeness to mythical goblins that appear in the country's folklore.

8 The ancient Japanese also **worshipped a god** known as the **shark man,** who was said to turn wind and rain into **violent typhoons.**

Australian Aboriginal art showing a shark and other native animals

SHARKS IN FOLKLORE

9 **American Indian tribes** of the Pacific Northwest in the United States and British Columbia in Canada include **elaborate carvings of sharks** on their **totem poles.**

10 The Nuu-chah-nulth, a Native tribe of Western Vancouver Island in Canada, tell stories of **Dogfish Mothers**—giant shark monsters who lived in deep holes under cliffs and liked to **eat canoes.**

11 These **fictional monsters** were likely inspired by real-life **great white sharks** that would hunt sea lions in the nearby waters.

12 Long ago, Native tribes of the **Marshall Islands** in the Pacific Ocean believed in **sacred sharks that protected fishers.**

13 **Māori mythology** of New Zealand tells of a god who placed a shark **high up in the sky,** forming what we know as the **Milky Way.**

14 When a family member passed away, some **Indigenous Polynesians** cast their loved one's body into the ocean to transform them into **shark spirits.**

15 To keep them safe while swimming, **pearl divers in Sri Lanka** first visited **"shark charmers"**—people thought to have **special, calming powers** over sharks.

15 POWERFUL

1 Sharks with sawlike jaws lived on Earth 60 million years **before tree forests—** and 170 million years **before dinosaurs—**even existed.

2 Many modern sharks are almost **identical to ancient species** from 150 million years ago.

3 Frilled sharks, for example, have changed very little since they **first appeared 95 million years ago.**

4 Fossil evidence suggests that **sharks' ancestors** may have existed as far back as 450 million years ago.

5 The **oldest known sharks** have been identified from scales found in rocks almost **455 million years old.**

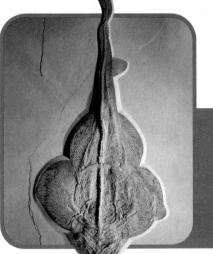

6 Some **65 species of prehistoric sharks** have been uncovered in the 318-million-year-old Bear Gulch Limestone in Montana, U.S.A.

7 From about 200 million to 150 million years ago, the area of **Solnhofen in Bavaria,** Germany, was home to early sharks that **resembled today's angel sharks.**

8 In 2019, researchers discovered the remains of a **shark with tiny thin, needlelike teeth.** The shark was found in a **clay pit** at Aiken, South Carolina, U.S.A., and was from 30 million years ago.

PREHISTORIC SHARKS

9 A fossil of *Cretoxyrhina mantelli*, **an extinct type of mackerel shark,** shows the fish lived about **100 to 70 million years ago** and measured up to 26 feet (8 m) long.

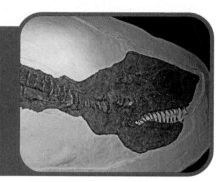

10 The oldest known **intact shark skeleton**—that of *Doliodus problematicus*—was found in Canada in 2003. The shark lived **409 million years ago.**

11 Experts say some prehistoric sharks feasted on **giant flying reptiles called pterosaurs.**

12 The **aptly named crusher shark,** which roamed the waters 100 to 85 million years ago, had **powerful jaws and more than 550 giant flattened teeth** used to crush shellfish.

13 Measuring more than **36 feet (11 m) long,** the crusher shark is the largest known **shellfish-eating animal ever.**

14 The **filter-feeding spiny shark**—which swam around some 400 million years ago—is one of the **first documented animals to have a jaw.**

15 The **peculiar-looking anvil shark,** nicknamed the "ironing board shark," sported a **flat, circular fin on its head,** topped with a **brushlike surface.**

comparison of a tooth of a great white shark (left) and a tooth of the extinct megalodon, the biggest shark ever

1 Sharks are often thought of as MINDLESS HUNTERS, when in fact they can be CURIOUS AND INTELLIGENT.

2 A shark's—and other vertebrates'—BRAIN SIZE compared to its body size is a rough measure of its INTELLIGENCE.

3 In general, the lower the brain-body ratio, the higher the INTELLIGENCE. The average shark ratio is about 1 to 750.

4 HUMANS have a brain-body ratio of about 1 to 50. Humans are MORE INTELLIGENT.

5 Still, a SHARK'S BRAIN compared to its body size is bigger than in all BONY FISH.

6 Sharks have LEARNED TO CONNECT sounds, light, and symbols with FOOD REWARDS in 10 or more tries.

7 GREAT WHITE sharks can nod their heads and ARCH their bodies to communicate.

8 Sharks can be TRAINED LIKE DOGS to touch a target or GRAB A PIECE OF FOOD.

9 A biologist in Germany trained gray bamboo-sharks to PUSH THEIR SNOUTS into squares on a screen to GET FOOD.

10 The biologist also trained the sharks to successfully NAVIGATE A MAZE, using colored walls and shapes to GUIDE THEM.

11 The bamboosharks were ABLE TO REMEMBER the path of the maze for UP TO SIX WEEKS.

12 A shark's LONG-TERM MEMORY may help it find food, avoid enemies, and LOCATE MATES in the ocean.

13 Studies show lemon sharks LEARN TO RESPOND to a flashing light 80 TIMES FASTER than cats do.

14 Some FEMALE SHARKS return to their birthplace, again and again, to GIVE BIRTH.

A great white shark uses pit sensors in its snout to find food.

35 SMART FACTS ABOUT

15 Most of a shark's brain deals with MOVEMENT and SENSORY DATA, like VISION and SMELL.

16 A DEEP-SEA SHARK'S BRAIN has a large region for SMELL and ELECTRORECEPTION, helping it navigate murky waters.

17 Slow, BOTTOM-DWELLING SHARKS tend to have the SMALLEST of shark brains.

18 The parts of the brain dedicated to LEARNING are SMALL in sharks.

19 Still, sharks have REMARKABLE MEMORIES and in experiments have been TRAINED TO RECOGNIZE shapes and colors.

20 At the SHEDD AQUARIUM in Chicago, Illinois, U.S.A., sharks are trained to come to eat at the sound of a DINNER BELL.

21 SHORTFIN MAKOS have learned how to distinguish between DIFFERENT SHAPES that reward them with fish treats.

22 In one study, Port Jackson sharks learned to associate LED LIGHTS with food DROPPED INTO THEIR TANK.

23 When researchers SHINED A LIGHT into the tank, the sharks searched for food, even 40 days after their LAST TEST.

24 Each year, gray reef sharks tend to use their SUPER MEMORY to return to the SAME PLACE at the SAME TIME to hunt.

25 Lemon sharks are known to PICK UP SPECIFIC BEHAVIORS from other sharks.

26 First, researchers TAUGHT a lemon shark to BUMP A TARGET with its nose to receive food.

27 When paired with a shark that DIDN'T KNOW THE SKILL, the new shark LEARNED to bump the target, too.

28 Using FOOD AS A REWARD, Port Jackson sharks have been trained to identify JAZZ MUSIC UNDERWATER.

29 The sharks were trained to go to SPEAKERS playing jazz music and not speakers playing CLASSICAL MUSIC.

30 Some scientists think the REGULAR BEAT of jazz music is closer to the NATURAL SOUNDS sharks are familiar with.

31 Captive nurse sharks have been trained to PICK UP HOOPS and bring them to their TRAINERS.

32 The sharks have also been trained to ROLL ONTO THEIR BACKS so vets can easily EXAMINE THEM.

33 In one study, researchers trained ZEBRA SHARKS to be picked up out of the water.

34 Caribbean reef sharks in the wild have been trained by scientists to HUNT LIONFISH.

35 By learning to eat lionfish, the REEF SHARKS help remove an invasive species that kills CORAL REEFS.

SHARK INTELLIGENCE

1 Most sharks serve as a **moving buffet for tiny parasites** that feast on everything from their skin to **undigested food in their bellies.**

2 A parasite is defined as any living organism that **lives on another living organism,** depending on its **host for food.**

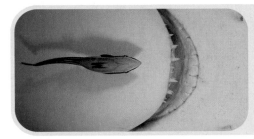

3 Some **1,500 species of parasites** are known to cling to **sharks, skates, and rays.**

4 Parasites are found all over a shark's body, from its skin to its jaws, as well as in its major organs, including the stomach, brain, and heart.

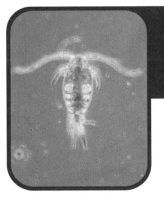

5 Small, shrimplike parasites called **copepods** cling to sharks' denticles, and are found in their **mouths and nasal cavities,** too.

6 While a shark's rough skin is designed to **deter unwanted guests,** some parasites have adapted to get **between** and **underneath** their dermal denticles.

7 One type of copepod **specifically targets** the Greenland shark's eyeballs, feeding on the surface of the **cornea.**

8 A shark with a parasite living in its eyeballs may go blind, but it will still be able to hunt successfully using its other senses.

SHARK PARASITES

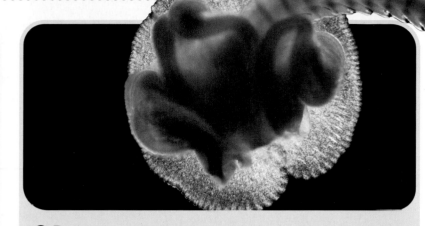

a close-up view of a parasitic copepod that lives in some shark species

9 **Parasitic tapeworms** have been found taking up residence in **sharks' stomachs.**

10 Scientists think **larvae** of the tapeworms **enter a shark's stomach** when it eats crustaceans and other fish **infested with them.**

11 Species including the gray nurse shark have been seen **scraping themselves along the seabed** to remove **skin parasites.**

12 One species of **parasitic barnacles** attaches itself to lanternsharks and **sucks out nutrients** from the sharks' flesh.

13 **Tongue-eating louse females** attach themselves to the tongue of species such as the **tiger shark.** The male lice attach themselves to the shark's gills.

14 Monogeneans are **types of flatworms** that live in the **gills of the bigeye sixgill shark**—and on no other species.

15 **Sea lampreys** are parasitic fish that can grow to be up to two feet (0.6 m) long while **living inside a shark's gut.**

1 The catchy kids' tune "**BABY SHARK**" inspired a shark-themed breakfast cereal.

2 The 2015 video for "**BABY SHARK**" has racked up more than 3.4 BILLION VIEWS on YouTube.

3 You can buy a "Baby Shark"—themed BASEBALL BAT. The song plays when you open the bat's box.

4 *SHARKNADO* IS A 2013 MOVIE ABOUT A **WATERSPOUT** THAT LIFTS SHARKS OUT OF THE **PACIFIC OCEAN** AND CARRIES THEM TO LAND.

5

DURING THE 2015 **Super Bowl halftime show,** COSTUME-WEARING BACKUP DANCER "left shark" BECAME AN INSTANT CELEBRITY.

25 POP-UP FACTS ABOUT

6 In the book *Harry Potter and the Goblet of Fire*, a character **CASTS A SPELL** on himself that turns his **HEAD** into that of a shark.

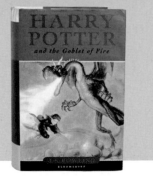

7 A CASINO IN LAS VEGAS, NEVADA, U.S.A., HAS A SWIMMING POOL WRAPPED AROUND A giant fish tank, SO YOU FEEL LIKE YOU'RE swimming with sharks.

8

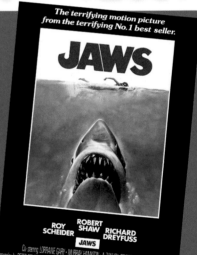

The movie *JAWS* is based on a book about the **TRUE-LIFE EVENTS** of a shark swimming off the coast of New Jersey, U.S.A., in 1916.

9 In *Jaws*, the shark **DOESN'T FULLY APPEAR ON-SCREEN** until 1 hour and 21 minutes into the two-hour movie.

10

"**DAMIEN HIRST LOOKING FOR SHARKS**" was an inflatable exhibit at the **SCULPTURE FOR SEA** event in Sydney, Australia, in 2018.

11 The **REALITY-TV SHOW** *Shark Tank* features people with small businesses attempting to sell their ideas to a **PANEL OF "SHARKS."**

12 IN **BUSINESS,** A "SHARK" REFERS TO SOMEONE WHO IS ESPECIALLY AGGRESSIVE AND **COMPETITIVE.**

13 In the movie *Finding Nemo*, the character **BRUCE**, a great white shark, is a softy who just wants to **MAKE NEW FRIENDS**.

14 A **SHARPEDO**, A POPULAR POKÉMON CHARACTER, HAS SHARK FANGS THAT **GROW BACK** IMMEDIATELY IF THEY **SNAP OFF**.

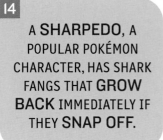

15 Diners at Ithaa—an **UNDER-THE-SEA RESTAURANT** in the Maldives—eat their meals while sharks **SWIM OVERHEAD**.

16 The 2004 animated movie **SHARK TALE** centers around Lenny, a young shark who wants to be a **VEGETARIAN** among a family of meat-eaters.

17 A shark nicknamed **MAXINE** became famous after being caught and injured in a net. Viewers watched her **RECOVER** in a South African aquarium.

SHARKS IN POP CULTURE

18 **A SHARK HEAD ENTRANCE** greets customers at a store in **BILOXI**, Mississippi, U.S.A.

19 YOU CAN RIDE A WATERSLIDE THROUGH A **HIDDEN SHARK TANK** AT A WATER PARK IN THE CANARY ISLANDS OFF THE WEST COAST OF AFRICA.

20 A 1970s cartoon called "**JABBERJAW**" follows the lives of a **GOOFY, DRUM-PLAYING SHARK** and his friends.

21 THE COMIC BOOK VILLAIN **TIGER SHARK** WAS ONCE AN OLYMPIC SWIMMER WHO HAD HIS GENES SPLICED WITH A SHARK'S TO GIVE HIM **AMPHIBIOUS SUPERPOWERS**.

22 One of the weapons used by JINX, a character in the fantasy game League of Legends, uses a **ROCKET LAUNCHER** shaped like a shark.

23 A **HOUSE** in Da Lat, Vietnam, that is open to tourists has a floor painted to look like the sea with a **SHARK**.

24 PHOTOS of sharks have graced the cover of *Time* magazine at least **THREE TIMES**. Of all the other animals, only **DOGS** have been featured more often.

25 AT CHRISTMASTIME, DIVERS DRESSED AS **SANTA CLAUS** DELIVER GOODIES TO THE **RESIDENT SHARKS** AT THE BUDAPEST AQUARIUM IN HUNGARY.

71

1 With about **120 species**, dogfish sharks make up the **second largest order** among sharks.

2 The dogfish family includes both **tiny sharks**, like the dwarf lanternshark, and **big ones**, like the Greenland shark.

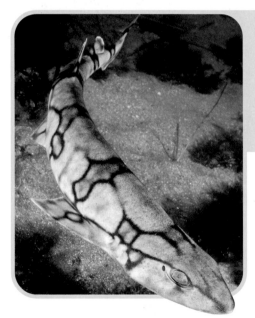

3 Dogfish sharks are found **all over the world** in different parts of the ocean, although many species are **bottom-dwellers**.

4 The spiny dogfish is named for its **two very sharp spines** (one on each dorsal fin), which serve as **defense against predators**.

5 There are more spiny dogfish— also known as **spurdogs** or **piked dogfish**—swimming in the seas than any other shark.

6 An estimated **535 million spiny dogfish** live off the Atlantic coast of Canada alone, with another **two billion** found off the Pacific coasts of Canada and the United States.

7 The dogfish's spines are **venomous** and can harm **anything that touches them.**

a lesser spotted dogfish in shallow water off the Isle of Man in the United Kingdom

DOGFISH SHARKS

8 As their name suggests, smooth dogfish sharks, also known as **smooth hound sharks,** do not have any spikes on their **dorsal fins.**

9 Unlike most sharks, smooth dogfish have rows of **flat, dull teeth** rather than sharp blades—perfect for crushing and chewing **crustaceans** and **mollusks.**

10 Smooth dogfish sharks **grow faster** and **produce more young** than many other sharks.

11 A smooth dogfish has **special pigment cells** in its skin, allowing it to change color to **blend into its surroundings.**

12 The Cuban dogfish is also known as the **puppyshark dogfish.**

13 Dogfish hunt **small fish, jellyfish, clams, krill,** and **octopuses** in large schools of up to 1,000 sharks.

14 A social media hashtag has sparked conversation and raised awareness about **dogfish conservation.**

15 The **prickly dogfish,** which lives in deep seas off the coasts of New Zealand and Australia, gets its name from its **super rough scales.**

1 THE FIVE-FOOT (1.5-M)-LONG **LEOPARD SHARK IS SPOTTED** LIKE ITS NAMESAKE.

2 Scientists say some 10 percent of sharks are **LUMINOUS,** which means their skin **GLOWS IN THE DARK.**

3 The luminous smalleye pygmy shark's **BELLY GLOWS BLUE,** a feature that helps it **BLEND IN** with the water.

4 THE TINY PYGMY LANTERN- SHARK IS COVERED WITH **glow-in-the-dark slime** THAT MIGHT HELP IT ATTRACT PREY.

glowing skin

5 THE LANTERNSHARK'S LIGHT ALSO HELPS IT BLEND INTO THE **RAYS OF SUNLIGHT** THAT STREAM INTO SHALLOW WATER.

25

AWESOME FACTS ABOUT

6 The velvet belly lanternshark has **GLOWING LIGHT SABER– LIKE SPINES** that may be used to ward off predators.

7

When threatened, a swell shark doubles in size by gulping water. Once safe, it makes a doglike bark and burps out water.

8 The goblin shark—which lives in the **PITCH-DARK DEPTHS** of the ocean—has a long snout, called a **ROSTRUM,** which extends from the top of its head.

9 The size of a goblin shark's snout gets smaller as it ages.

10 THE GREENLAND SHARK HAS **POISONOUS FLESH.**

11 A goblin shark's **LONG AND SCRAGGLY TEETH** stick out even when its **MOUTH IS CLOSED.**

12 A special substance in a dogfish shark's skin protects it from picking up **VIRAL INFECTIONS.**

13  The epaulette shark can **SLOW ITS BREATHING** and **HEART RATE** enough to survive 60 times longer **WITHOUT OXYGEN** than humans can.

14 The epaulette shark will sometimes climb out of the ocean at low tide and "WALK" ON ITS FINS between tide pools to hunt stranded prey.

15 SHARKS don't enter deep sleep LIKE HUMANS DO. THEY BECOME SEMICONSCIOUS WHEN AT REST.

16 The eyes of a porbeagle shark have a **SPECIAL RETINA** that detects movement of objects extremely well when it is on the hunt.

17 The **SKIN** of an adult whale shark is as thick as a **MATTRESS**.

SHARK FEATURES

18 Fish, including sharks, **DO NOT HAVE VOCAL CORDS**, but they can make **SOUNDS** by moving various **PARTS OF THEIR BODY**.

19  Female hammerheads sometimes do **FLIPS AND TWISTS WHILE SWIMMING**— movements that may be used to communicate with other sharks.

20 IF A SHARK IS FLIPPED UPSIDE DOWN, IT GOES INTO A **SLEEPY, ZOMBIE-LIKE STATE** CALLED TONIC IMMOBILITY.

21  Scientists use tonic immobility **TO CALM SHARKS** for studies. When the sharks are flipped back, they wake up and **START SWIMMING AGAIN**.

22 A tiger shark is born with **GRAY SPOTS** that turn into **BARS** as the shark grows.

23 The bars **FADE** as the shark ages and are **BARELY VISIBLE** in full-grown adults.

24 The prickly shark has **TWO DORSAL FINS OF EQUAL SIZE** and no anal fin.

25 THE SAWBACK ANGEL SHARK IS THE ONLY ONE OF ITS KIND TO HAVE **SPINES RUNNING DOWN ITS BACK.**

75

❶ In a 2012 show featuring **high-end Givenchy fashion**, models walked the runway wearing oversize **shark-tooth necklaces.**

❷ The **body shape, teeth,** and **skin** of sharks have inspired designers of everything from **clothes, jewelry, buildings,** and **cars** to **furniture.**

❸ One company sells **high-heel pumps** featuring a graphic of a shark with **scary, sharp teeth and beady eyes.**

❹ The sneaker company Vans released a line of shoes in shark print—with part of the proceeds going to a charity supporting the world's oceans.

❺ Adidas also released a version of a **shark sneaker,** complete with "gill slits" on the sides that open to offer **extra ventilation** when you walk.

❻ The Adidas **SHARKS** sneaker also has a ruby red inner lining to represent the color of a shark's gums.

❼ **Car designers** have copied the streamline shape of sharks to give their vehicles the look of **high speed** on the road.

SHARK-INSPIRED STYLE

8 For about $150, you can buy a necklace with an actual tiger shark tooth cast in sterling silver.

9 The "sharkini" bathing suit's midsection is trimmed with triangular teeth made to look like a shark's fierce chompers.

10 An Australian jewelry designer creates delicate shark-shaped necklaces and earrings with the aim of squashing violent stereotypes about the fish.

11 At Fashion Week in Paris, France, in 2019, several models carried shark shoulder bags in a variety of materials and designs.

12 A Japanese company makes the Shark Cushion Bed, which looks like an upside-down shark. You enter the jaws to sleep in the shark's belly.

13 For a pet pup, you can buy a cuddly shark costume.

14 You can have a seat in the Great Grey Shark Chair, featuring teeth made of white leather, fin-shape legs, and two fluffy fish cushions.

15 Sharkskin suits are made from a smooth, somewhat shiny fabric that's said to look like the skin of a shark.

The bow of this Russian Arctic ship has a shark's jaw marking—a symbol of how it cuts through the ice.

77

1 Some species of sharks migrate through **all the oceans.**

2 Sharks typically migrate to find **food,** warm or cold water, and **mates.**

3 Sharks also migrate to find good locations **to have pups.**

4 A shark may rely on **fat stored in its liver** to give it **energy** as it travels long distances.

5 Sharks have one of four **migratory patterns**—local, coastal pelagic, highly pelagic, and diadromous.

6 **"Pelagic"** comes from a Greek word meaning **"open sea"**—neither close to the ocean bed nor near shores.

7 **"Diadromous"** refers to migrating between sea and fresh water. It comes from Greek words meaning **"through running."**

8 **Local sharks,** like the nurse shark, stay within some 100 miles (161 km) of the same spot **throughout their life.**

9 **Coastal pelagic sharks** follow food and usually **stick close to shores** as they migrate.

10 Coastal pelagic sharks, including the **oceanic blacktip, tiger,** and **sandbar sharks,** migrate some 1,000 miles (1,600 km) each year.

11 Blue sharks and mako sharks are **highly pelagic,** migrating into the open sea and traveling the **farthest of all sharks.**

12 Some of the **fastest sharks** are highly pelagic, migrating some **37 miles (60 km) a day.**

13 Scientists use **GPS tags** to track sharks' movements as they migrate.

14 Knowing where sharks travel helps us **protect** them.

15 One **tagged mako shark** nicknamed Carol was clocked migrating **62 miles (99.8 km) in a day.**

16 In six months, **Carol** covered **8,265 miles (13,300 km)**— the distance between the United States and the Philippines.

17 Another mako shark, **nicknamed Hell's Bay,** swam more than **13,000 miles (20,900 km) in 600 days.**

18 Great white sharks migrating from **South Africa** to **Australia** travel 6,900 miles (11,100 km) in about 100 days.

19 The great white's migration is like swimming the distance of the United States **from coast to coast—twice!**

20 Other great whites migrate between warm waters off **San Francisco, California,** and **Hawai'i**—a 2,280-mile (3,670-km) journey.

21 **Halfway** between San Francisco and Hawai'i, many of the sharks **stop** at a feeding area nicknamed the **"white shark café."**

migrating nurse sharks

50
MOVING Facts About
SHARK MIGRATION

22
The "café" is a huge patch of ocean rich in **phytoplankton, fish, squid,** and **jellyfish.**

23
At the café, the sharks perform **vertical migration,** diving as deep as **2,900 feet (884 m)** to seek out food.

24
Great white sharks have been tracked **diving** to **1,400 feet (427 m)** during the day.

25
At night, great white sharks come back to **650 feet (198 m)** below the surface.

26
The great white's vertical migration appears to be timed with the **day's light cycle.**

27
Migrating great white sharks have been spotted **riding giant eddies,** or swirling currents, to help them **reach food sources faster.**

28
Tagged blue **sharks** make regular trips between **New York, U.S.A.,** and **Brazil** or from **Virginia, U.S.A.,** to **Portugal.**

29
Experts once tracked a salmon shark **11,321 miles (18,219 km)** over **631 days.**

30
That shark's journey of almost **half the distance around Earth** is one of the longest ever recorded.

31
Some **hammerhead sharks** migrate about 1,800 miles (2,900 km) to the same spots every year.

32
A favorite **great hammerhead** destination is the **Bahamas,** where they gather each winter.

33
One tagged spiny dogfish swam over 5,000 miles (8,050 km) from **Washington State, U.S.A.,** to **Japan.**

34
The whale shark is among the ocean's most widely traveled creatures, with individuals migrating more than 12,400 miles (20,000 km) in two years.

35
A whale shark nicknamed Anne was once tracked swimming from the **Galápagos Islands** across the Pacific Ocean to **Asia.**

36
Each year, **blacktip reef sharks** swim up the coast of Florida as the **biggest known migration of sharks.**

37
Scientists flying in planes above the migrating sharks have recorded up to **14,000 individuals.**

38
Drones are now used to **track** and **count** migrating sharks from above.

39
In California, researchers are using **artificial intelligence** to help interpret the drone images and **better identify sharks.**

40
The information could one day be used to **alert lifeguards** on beaches about sharks in the water.

41
Thresher sharks appear to remember their **shortest migration routes.**

42
The tiger shark may have a **"mental map"** of its ocean area in its brain.

43
Scientists have **tracked** tiger sharks traveling over **4,660 miles (7,500 km)** from the North Atlantic Ocean to the Caribbean Sea and back.

44
A speedy great **white shark** once covered some **74 miles (119 km) a day** during migration.

45
The **average speed** of some other sharks is around **56 miles (90 km) a day.**

46
Rising ocean temperatures due to **climate change** may be making sharks migrate into new territories to seek cooler waters.

47
For example, blacktip sharks have been spotted off the **coast of Long Island,** New York.

48
This migration is **50 percent farther north** than expected for the blacktip shark.

49
In 2019, scientists in **Australia** safely attached **Fitbit trackers** to migrating Port Jackson sharks.

50
The **Fitbit** data revealed a **932-mile (1,500-km)** migration that the scientists never knew the sharks made.

❶ A person who **studies marine fish**, including sharks, rays, and skates, is known as an **ichthyologist**.

❷ "Ichthyology" comes from the Greek words for **"fish"** (*ichthys*) and **"study"** (*logos*).

❸ **Eugenie Clark**, a famous U.S. ichthyologist, was known as **"The Shark Lady."** Born in 1922, she did extensive work with sharks, especially lemon sharks.

SHARK REPELLENT

GROSS WEIGHT - 115 GRAMS

INSTRUCTIONS:
1. TEAR OPEN OUTER FOIL BAG
2. TIE INNER BAG TO PERSON
3. SQUEEZE IN WATER TO PRODUCE BLACK CLOUD
   IN CENTRE OF CLOUD

❹ One of Clark's **biggest contributions?** Proving that sharks are **smart** and can **learn through training**. They are not dumb and deadly.

❺ Clark also discovered the **first effective shark repellent**, made from the natural chemicals of a **flatfish**.

❻ The *Squalus clarkae* shark—also known as **Genie's dogfish**—is named after Clark.

❼ Frenchman **Jacques Cousteau**—one of the most well-known **ocean explorers** in history—was a shark specialist and among the very first experts to focus on **shark tagging** and **sharks' migratory patterns**.

❽ Famous for his **filmmaking**, Cousteau was also one of the first people to capture sharks swimming underwater for his **nature documentaries**, which premiered in the late 1960s.

Scientists measure the length of a Caribbean reef shark in the wild.

SHARK EXPERTS

9 In a first-of-its-kind experiment, **National Geographic Explorer Gibbs Kuguru** and **shark biologist Ryan Johnson** confirmed that sharks off the coast of South Africa have a "camo-mode."

10 Using a fake seal as bait, **Kuguru and Johnson** drew sharks out of the water, then compared their coloration against a nearby board with **white, gray, and black panels.**

11 Kuguru and Johnson discovered that **great white sharks** might be able to change their own coloration, which could help them better ambush their prey.

12 **Hans and Lotte Hass** were an Austrian husband-and-wife team of underwater filmmakers working in the 1950s. Lotte Hass was the first diver to film whale sharks and manta rays **in the wild.**

13 Photographer **Brian Skerry** has made more than **14 trips around the world** to take pictures of shark species, including the tiger shark, great white shark, oceanic whitetip shark, and shortfin mako shark.

14 All told, Skerry has spent more than **10,000 hours underwater** snapping pictures of sharks.

15 Many shark experts speak out about **protecting these fish** and how sharks **aren't as scary as they seem.**

1 The deep-dwelling **viper dogfish** is so rare, only a handful of specimens have been studied since it was **first discovered in 1986.**

2 Described as **"alien-like"** with **glassy, black skin** and **spiky, spaced-out teeth,** the viper dogfish swallows its prey whole.

3 There have been **fewer than 300 confirmed sightings** of the **megamouth shark.**

Seeing a stingray is rare because a camouflaged stingray can be hard to find.

4 The megamouth is so rare that scientists first thought to classify it in a new genus and family when they discovered it in 1976.

5 One of the **world's rarest sharks,** *Squatina squatina*—a type of **angel shark**—is found almost exclusively near the **Canary Islands** off the west coast of Africa.

6 In 2019, a six-foot (1.8-m) *Squatina squatina* was spotted off the Welsh coast in the United Kingdom—the first time the shark had been seen in British waters in some 50 years.

7 In 2005, fishers in Australia spotted a **frilled shark**—which looks more like an **eel** or a **snake** than a shark—a species very rarely seen in its natural environment.

8 Scientists recently spotted a **Broken Ridge skate** on a seamount in the **southern Indian Ocean**—only the second of its kind ever spotted and scientifically recorded.

SKATES, AND RAYS

9 Until the late 2010s the **Pondicherry shark**, which can survive in both salt water and fresh water, was considered a **"lost shark"** because no one had seen any since 1979.

10 A recent quest to find the small stocky, gray shark led to a potential Pondicherry sighting in a river close to a remote fishing village in Sri Lanka.

11 The elusive whitespotted wedgefish—a type of ray found in Australian and Asian waters—is known as the **guitar shark** by locals for its **long, flat body** and three distinct **shark-like fins**.

12 The last sighting of a **honeycomb catshark** was reported back in the 1970s in the western Indian Ocean, near **South Africa**.

13 It was only in 2006 that the honeycomb catshark was formally named—for its **funky patterned skin**—and considered a **species of its own**.

14 **Scuba divers** swimming off the coast of Mozambique are helping scientists track smalleyes by taking **videos** or **pictures** of them.

15 The **smalleye stingray**—which can grow to be wider than a **king-size bed**—is the largest of all marine rays, but it's also the **most mysterious**, and is very rarely spotted alive.

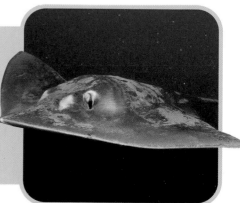

1
Shark numbers have **sharply decreased** recently.

2
In fact, almost half of shark species have **suffered serious declines** in population over the past 100 years.

3
About **26 known species of sharks**—about 20 percent of all sharks—are in **danger of extinction.**

4
People are a bigger danger to sharks than sharks are to people.

5
Humans are responsible for the death of about **100 million sharks** every year.

6
Over 100 species of sharks are targeted each year for their **fins, meat, liver, oil, gills, teeth, cartilage,** and **skin.**

7
Shark finning is the act of catching sharks, **cutting off their fins,** and throwing the sharks back into the water.

8
Because sharks **can't swim without their fins,** they cannot survive having their fins removed.

9
Shark finning happens all over the world, but mostly in the waters of the **Pacific** and **Indian Oceans.**

10
Shark finning is **banned** or **restricted** in almost 60 countries—including the United States—but it is also **hard to regulate.**

11
In some countries, eating **shark fin soup** is a sign of wealth.

12
Served at **weddings** and banquets in Asia, shark fin soup can cost up to **$100 a bowl.**

13
Shark fin is used in soup for **its texture, not its taste.** The soup actually gets its flavor from **chicken** or **ham broth.**

14
Just **one pound** (454 g) **of shark fins** can sell for $450.

15
Large fins from basking or whitetip reef sharks can sell for **thousands of dollars.**

16
Skates and **rays** are also targeted for their fins.

17
Shark liver oil is sometimes used in **cosmetics** and other everyday products.

18
A 2019 study testing 24 **beauty products** found traces of **shark DNA** in 12.5 percent of them.

19
Shark DNA also appeared in **63 percent of pet foods** tested in the same study.

20
Shark skin is used to make such **luxury leather** items as boots, shoes, handbags, wallets, and belts.

21
The **skin is taken** from the tiger, lemon, dusky, nurse, sandbar, porbeagle, shortfin mako, blue, and bull shark species.

a group of lemon sharks

50 ALARMING FACTS ABOUT THREATS TO SHARKS

22
The skin of stingrays, *Dasyatis* species, is also used to make leather goods.

23
Overfishing— taking more fish from the sea than can be replaced naturally by breeding—is a serious threat to sharks' future.

24
Many shark species are particularly vulnerable to overfishing as they reproduce slowly.

25
Bycatch—when fish become caught accidentally in nets meant for other species—kills some 12 million sharks every year.

26
Many sharks captured through bycatch are also finned by fishers.

27
It's estimated that dusky shark populations in the Atlantic Ocean have declined by 85 percent due to bycatch.

28
The daggernose shark is endangered because it gets caught in nets used to catch small coastal fish on which it feeds.

29
The scalloped hammerhead's large head makes it more likely to get caught in a fishing net.

30
Sharks also fall victim to "longlining"—the use of long fishing lines strung with thousands of baited hooks to catch fish like tuna.

31
When sharks feed on the fish on the lines, they may get stuck on the hooks and die.

32
As many as one in every five fish caught on longlines is a shark.

33
For blue sharks and shortfin makos, almost two-thirds of their territories are affected by longlines.

34
Almost one-quarter of the ocean area used by all sharks is exposed to longline fishing.

35
Longline fishing has been banned from shark areas around the Bahamas and along parts of the Pacific coast of North America.

36
Ocean pollution and warming ocean temperatures are additional threats to sharks—and to the fish they eat to survive.

37
These threats, as well as illegal diving and damage to coral reefs, endanger those sharks that feed on tiny reef animals.

38
Ocean pollutants, such as pesticides farmers use on their crops, can wash into oceans through rainwater, affecting marine life including sharks.

39
Rare sightings of tumors on sharks have raised concerns that pollution is making the animals sick.

40
People catch blue sharks for their cartilage, which contains chondroitin, a drug used to treat ailments like arthritis.

41
Dogfish are commonly fished for their meat, which is sometimes called rock salmon, huss, or flake in restaurants.

42
Dogfish meat is often used in the popular fish and chips dish, especially in Europe.

43
In a 2019 study of U.K. fish-and-chip shops, nearly 90 percent were selling the endangered spiny dogfish.

44
The nursehound shark, considered a "near threatened" species, is also used in fish and chips.

45
Fishers in the town of Chatham, Massachusetts, U.S.A., caught about six million pounds (2.7 million kg) of dogfish in one year.

46
Sawfish—which are types of rays— are now considered the world's most threatened species.

47
Scientists estimate that sawfish have declined by over 90 percent of their original numbers.

48
Of the five species of sawfish, just two are protected by the Endangered Species Act.

49
It is illegal to catch or trade any protected fish, but people break laws, so sharks are not safe everywhere they swim.

50
"Lost sharks"— small species that because they pose no threat to people are little studied— are among the most endangered.

1 While sharks **face many threats**, the good news is that many people are working to protect the **most vulnerable species.**

2 Shark finning is **illegal** in about 100 countries, including **Trinidad and Tobago, New Zealand, United Arab Emirates, Australia, Palau, Canada,** and the **United States.**

3 Several locations, such as **Egypt, Fiji,** and many **U.S.** and **Canadian cities,** have also created **laws banning the sale of shark fins.**

4 New **"Fin Free" campaigns** in China and other parts of Asia are attempting to encourage people to **skip shark fin soup** on the menu.

5 Worldwide, nearly **60 airlines** and **container shipping companies** have agreed **not to transport shark fins** aboard their planes and ships.

6 In China, **shark fin consumption** has fallen by **80 percent** in the last decade.

It takes a spine to **Do Right By Dogfish!**

7 The Ocean Conservancy **"Do Right By Dogfish"** campaign in the North Atlantic, started in 2011, brought about **catch limits** for fishers, reducing overfishing of dogfish.

8 Signed into U.S. law in 2010, the **Shark Conservation Act** requires that all sharks caught in the United States be brought to shore **with their fins naturally attached.**

SAV OU SHAR SHAR

SAVING SHARKS

9 In July 2014, the **scalloped hammerhead** became the first shark species protected under the U.S. Endangered Species Law.

10 The state of California, U.S.A., has **cut back on bycatching** by banning the use of certain nets near the shore.

11 Researchers are looking into **changing the design** of fishing hooks and fishing lines to make it easier for sharks to **escape**—and **survive**—if they are caught on a longline.

12 In 2009, the **island country of Palau** in the western Pacific Ocean became the first to create a **shark sanctuary** by banning all shark fishing within the 240,000 square miles (621,597 sq km) of its waters.

13 **French Polynesia** and the **Cook Islands** in the South Pacific Ocean have since **banned all shark fishing** in their waters. **Mexico** doesn't allow shark fishing between May and August of each year.

14 In Florida, U.S.A., it's **illegal to "land" sharks,** meaning they must be returned to the water **free, alive,** and **unharmed** if caught.

15 Thanks to **conservation efforts,** the great white shark—once thought to be in decline—has seen a recent **population surge** in the Pacific Ocean.

Protesters at a beach in Sydney, Australia, speak out against the capturing and killing of sharks off Western Australia.

GLOSSARY

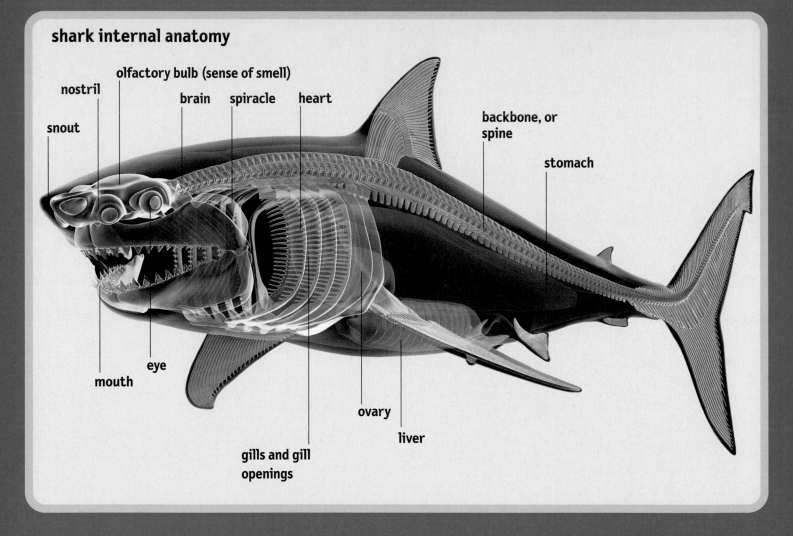

shark internal anatomy

olfactory bulb (sense of smell)

nostril

brain spiracle heart

snout

backbone, or
spine

stomach

eye

mouth

ovary

liver

gills and gill
openings

adaptation a special physical feature or a behavior that helps an animal survive

ampullae of Lorenzini special sense organs that run down a shark's body and allow it to detect faint electrical signals

barbels skinny, whiskerlike sensory organs near the mouth. Some sharks, like angel sharks, use barbels to detect prey.

biodiversity the variety of life in the world or in a particular habitat or ecosystem

bioluminescence an adaptation that allows an animal to create or use light for camouflage, to find food, attract a mate, or use as an alarm

breach to rise and break through the surface of the water

bycatch when fish such as sharks become accidentally caught in fishing nets meant for other species

camouflage color, pattern, and/or body shape that helps an animal hide or blend into its surroundings

capillaries tiny blood vessels that allow fish to absorb oxygen from water flowing over their gills and deliver it to their body

cartilage flexible but sturdy tissue that shapes our ears, our nose, and a shark's skeleton

caudal fin a fish's tail fin

cephalofoil the scientific name for the shape of a hammerhead shark's head

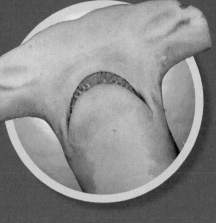
hammerhead shark

Chondrichthyes the class of cartilaginous fish that includes sharks, skates, rays, and chimaeras

class in taxonomy, a high-level grouping of organisms that have similar qualities. Sharks are in the class Chondrichthyes.

countershading a type of camouflage that, in sharks, is based on having dark skin on top and light skin underneath the body, making them less visible from below

defense a means by which an organism protects itself from attack or harm

dermal denticles tiny, toothlike scales that cover a shark's skin. Also known as placoid scales.

DNA the genetic material that carries all the information about how a living thing will look and function

dorsal fin a triangle-shaped fin on a shark's back

Elasmobranchii the subclass of cartilaginous fish that have five to seven visible gill openings; includes sharks, rays, and skates. (See pages 91 to 93 for the classification and evolution of Elasmobranchii.)

electroreception an organism's ability to pick up electrical signals from other living creatures. For sharks, it is regarded as their sixth sense.

embryo a baby animal developing inside an egg or female

endangered a plant or animal found in such small numbers that it is at risk of becoming extinct

finning the act of catching sharks, cutting off their fins, and throwing the sharks back into the water

fossil the preserved remains or traces of an organism that lived a long time ago

fossil shark tooth

habitat a living area or home of a collection of plants and animals

Holocephali the subclass of cartilaginous fish that have a single gill opening; includes chimaeras

---

shark fins

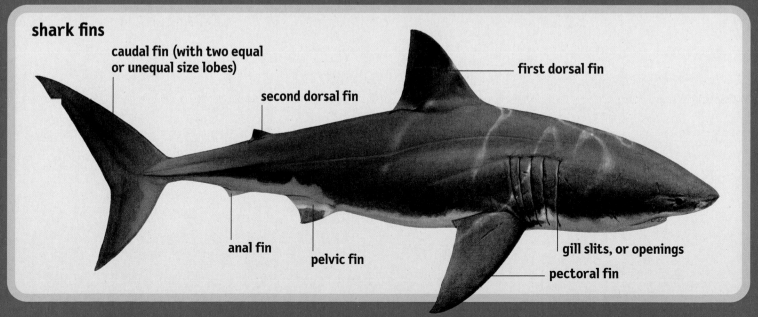

caudal fin (with two equal or unequal size lobes)

first dorsal fin

second dorsal fin

anal fin

pelvic fin

gill slits, or openings

pectoral fin

GLOSSARY (CONTINUED)

ichthyologist a person who studies marine fish, including sharks, rays, and skates

kingdom in taxonomy, the highest level of classification of living things

lateral line a canal filled with fluid that runs down each side of a shark's body

mermaid's purses

mermaid's purse the hard casing around the egg of a shark, skate, or chimaera

midnight zone a deep layer of the ocean that starts about 3,300 feet (1,005 m) down

migration the regular movement of an animal from one location to another

nares the two openings near a shark's snout, similar to human nostrils

oophagy the scientific name for animals feeding on unfertilized eggs while in their mother's womb

order in taxonomy, a mid-level grouping of organisms that are closely related to one another. An order is a subdivision of a class.

overfishing when fish are harvested from the sea at rates too high for them to replace themselves naturally by breeding

oviparous animals that lay eggs from which the young emerge

ovoviviparous animals whose young grow in eggs that hatch inside their mom's womb. The young are born live.

pectoral fins a pair of fins located behind a fish's head that help control motion in the water

pheromones natural chemicals produced by animals that attract members of the opposite sex of the same species

phylum in taxonomy, a high grouping of organisms that share similar characteristics. Sharks belong to the phylum Chordata.

plankton tiny organisms drifting or floating in the sea or fresh water

predator an animal that hunts and eats other animals

prey an animal that is eaten by another animal

plankton

pup a newborn or young shark

shiver a name for a group of sharks

species in taxonomy, the lowest level of grouping closely related organisms. Individuals of a species can breed and produce young.

spinal cord the large bundle or group of nerves running through the center of the spine. It carries messages between the brain and the rest of the body.

spiracle an opening on top of a shark's or ray's head that brings water over the gills

tagging attaching radio or satellite tags to an animal to track its movement

tapetum lucidum a layer of mirrored crystals behind the retina of each of a shark's eyes that helps the shark see in dark waters

taxonomy the science of naming, defining, and classifying groups of living things

tonic immobility a sleepy, zombie-like state that a shark enters if it is flipped upside down

shark tag

twilight zone the part of the ocean that is about 650 feet (198 m) down, where visibility is limited

vertebrates animals with a backbone and spinal cord

viviparous animals that give birth to live young

KINDS OF SHARKS

To keep track of the many different living things on Earth, scientists classify them into groups that are based on traits, or characteristics, they share. The largest—and most diverse—group is called a kingdom. The smallest group, called a species, includes members that are very closely related and can mate with one another. Use the chart and information below to keep track of these groups— and discover how sharks fit in.

CLASSIFICATION

Sharks are part of the class Chondrichthyes, which includes one grouping of fish that have a skeleton made of cartilage. Other cartilaginous fish are in the class Chondrostei and include sturgeons, gars, bichirs, and paddlefish.

Chondrichthyes is divided into two subclasses— Elasmobranchii (sharks, skates, and rays) and Holocephali (chimaera). Elasmobranchii has nine orders, grouped by similar physical characteristics. They are listed to the right and on page 92.

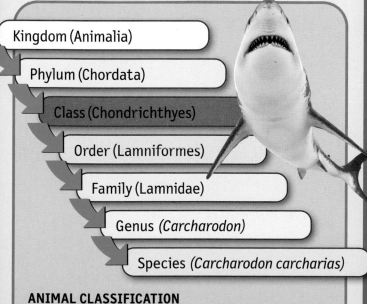

Kingdom (Animalia)

Phylum (Chordata)

Class (Chondrichthyes)

Order (Lamniformes)

Family (Lamnidae)

Genus (*Carcharodon*)

Species (*Carcharodon carcharias*)

ANIMAL CLASSIFICATION
The sequence of groupings above shows how the great white shark, *Carcharodon carcharias*, is placed within the animal kingdom.

Order Rajiformes

Common name
Skates and rays

Common characteristics
- flattened body
- large, winglike pectoral fins attached to the head
- long, narrow tail; often with a sharp barb
- gill slits on the underside of the body
- Order includes manta rays, eagle rays, guitarfish.

ray

Order Squatiniformes

Common name
Angel sharks

Common characteristics
- flattened body
- whiskerlike barbels near the mouth
- large, winglike pectoral fins along the body
- tail fin
- sets of five gill slits
- Order includes Pacific angel sharks, sawback angel sharks.

angel shark

Order Orectolobiformes

Common name
Carpet sharks

Common characteristics
- varied body shape
- whiskerlike barbels near the mouth
- patterned skin
- two dorsal fins
- sets of five gill slits
- Order includes wobbegongs, whale sharks, nurse sharks.

carpet shark

KINDS OF SHARKS (CONTINUED)

Order Squaliformes

Common name
Dogfish sharks

Common characteristics
- torpedo-shaped body
- mouth under the snout
- two dorsal fins
- sets of five gill slits
- Order includes spiny dogfish, lanternsharks, and Greenland sharks.

dogfish shark

Order Hexanchiformes

Common name
Frilled and cow sharks

Common characteristics
- large mouth that extends back past the eyes
- sets of six or seven gill slits
- tail and dorsal fins
- nicknamed "living fossils" because of their primitive-looking appearance
- Order includes broadnose sevengill sharks, frilled sharks.

cow shark

Order Heterodontiformes

Common name
Horn and bullhead sharks

Common characteristics
- hornlike brow ridges over the eyes
- sets of five gill slits
- fin spines
- toxic spines near the two dorsal fins
- Order includes Port Jackson sharks, zebra bullhead sharks.

Port Jackson shark

Order Lamniformes

Common name
Mackerel sharks

Common characteristics
- long snout and mouth
- sets of five gill slits
- generally large in size
- Order includes great white sharks, thresher sharks, mako sharks.

mako shark

Order Pristiophoriformes

Common name
Saw sharks

Common characteristics
- long, flat snout studded with teeth
- two long barbels hanging from the snout
- sets of five or six gill slits
- Order includes Japanese saw sharks, longnose saw sharks.

saw shark

Order Carcharhiniformes

Common name
Ground sharks

Common characteristics
- wide mouth with sharp-edged teeth
- two dorsal fins
- sets of five gill slits
- movable membrane over the eyes to protect them when the shark is feeding
- Order includes reef sharks, hammerhead sharks, catsharks.

scalloped hammerhead shark

SHARK EVOLUTION

The way that modern animals evolved from pre-historic ancestors is usually represented visually by an "evolutionary tree." The "branches" of the tree represent splits in the course of evolution based on certain body characteristics. With sharks, the first split is based on the presence or absence of an anal fin. The second splits are based on either body shape and position of the mouth, or on the numbers of gills and dorsal fins. There are further splits and branches based on a range of other characteristics. From fossil evidence, it is possible to determine when each split took place and when the existing orders of sharks first became established.

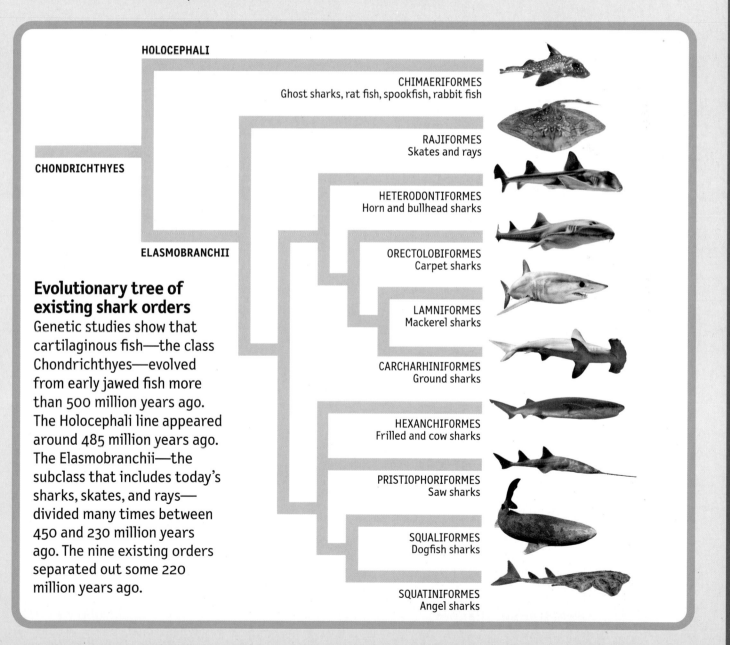

HOLOCEPHALI

CHIMAERIFORMES
Ghost sharks, rat fish, spookfish, rabbit fish

CHONDRICHTHYES

RAJIFORMES
Skates and rays

HETERODONTIFORMES
Horn and bullhead sharks

ELASMOBRANCHII

ORECTOLOBIFORMES
Carpet sharks

Evolutionary tree of existing shark orders

Genetic studies show that cartilaginous fish—the class Chondrichthyes—evolved from early jawed fish more than 500 million years ago. The Holocephali line appeared around 485 million years ago. The Elasmobranchii—the subclass that includes today's sharks, skates, and rays—divided many times between 450 and 230 million years ago. The nine existing orders separated out some 220 million years ago.

LAMNIFORMES
Mackerel sharks

CARCHARHINIFORMES
Ground sharks

HEXANCHIFORMES
Frilled and cow sharks

PRISTIOPHORIFORMES
Saw sharks

SQUALIFORMES
Dogfish sharks

SQUATINIFORMES
Angel sharks

INDEX

horn shark
pup

RESOURCES

Claybourne, Anna. *Sharks—Predators of the Sea.* Firefly Books, 2016.

DK Children. *Sharks and Other Deadly Ocean Creatures Visual Encyclopedia,* 2016.

DK Children. *Super Shark Encyclopedia,* 2015.

Helfman, Gene S., and George H. Burgess. *Sharks: The Animal Answer Guide.* Johns Hopkins Press, 2014.

McMillan, Beverly, and John A. Musick. *Sharks.* Simon & Schuster Books for Young Readers, 2008.

Musgrave, Ruth. *Everything Sharks.* National Geographic Kids, 2011.

Pringle, Laurence. *Sharks! Strange and Wonderful.* Boyds Mills Press, 2008.

Ramsey, Ocean, and Juan Oliphant. *What You Should Know About Sharks.* CreateSpace Independent Publisher, 2019.

Skerry, Brian. *The Ultimate Book of Sharks.* National Geographic Kids, 2018.

Skomal, Greg, and Nick Caloyianis. *The Shark Handbook.* Cider Mill Press, 2008.

CREDITS

Cover (background), Tracey Jones Photography/SS; (CTR), wildestanimal/Getty Images; (UP RT), Jeff Rotman/NPL;(skin), yoshio511/SS; (tooth, top), Mark_Kostich/SS; (tooth, bottom) chris kolaczan/SS; (LO LE), Franco Tempesta/(CTR LE), Christine/AS; (UP LE), Alastair Pollock/Getty Images; spine, Ryan M. Bolton/SS; back cover (LE), Kelvin Aitken/VWPics/ASP; (CTR), OutdoorWorks/SS; (RT), Dan Burton/NPL; 1 (skin, throughout), yoshio511/SS; 1, Chris & Monique Fallows/NPL; 2-3 (background, throughout), Tracey Jones Photography/SS; 3, R. Gino Santa Maria/AS; 4, frantisekhojdysz/SS; 5 (tooth, top), Mark_Kostich/SS; 5 (tooth, bottom), chris kolaczan/SS; 5 (CTR RT), Tatiana Belova/SS; 5 (LO), Andrea Izzotti/AS; 5 (CTR LE), Christine/AS; 6, Scubazoo/ASP; 7, wildestanimal/SS; 8-9 (background), Dream69/DR; 8 (1), Nikolai Sorokin/AS; 8 (2), Gerard Soury/Getty Images; 8 (3), Florian Graner/NPL; 8 (5), shizuruvten/AS; 9 (6), wildestanimal/SS; 9 (9), Naluphoto/DR; 9 (10), Doug Perrine/Blue Planet Archive; 10-11, NG Maps; 10 (1), Franco Banfi/Blue Planet Archive; 10 (2), Bruce Rasner/Rotman/NPL; 10 (3 & 4), wildestanimal/AS; 11 (5 & 6), wildestanimal/AS; 11 (7 & 8), Andrea Izzotti/AS; 11 (9), Vladimir Wrangel/AS; 11 (10), Kletr/AS; 12 (1), whitcomberd/AS; 12 (5), ia_64/AS; 12 (6), shanemyersphoto/AS; 12 (10), Hbuchholz/DR; 12 (11), Greg Amptman/DR; 13 (13), Norbert Wu/Minden Pictures; 13 (17), Chris Moncrieff/DR; 13 (18), Petr Zamecnik/DR; 13 (19), Doug Perrine/NPL; 13 (20), wildestanimal/SS; 13 (21), prochym/AS; 13 (23), Sabine/AS; 14-15 (background), David B. Fleetham/Blue Planet Archive; 14 (2), JackF/AS; 14 (16 & 20), Jeff Rotman/NPL; 14 (21), Nicolas Voisin/DR; 14 (30), Phanuwatn/DR; 14 (31), Alex Hyde/NPL; 15 (37), Jeremy Brown/DR; 15 (40), Pstonefy/AS; 16-17, Martin Prochazkacz/SS; 16 (1), Chumphon Whangchom/DR; 16 (3), Chrisalleaume/DR; 16 (5), Naluphoto/DR; 17 (8), Uryadnikov Sergey/AS; 17 (10), bennymarty/AS; 17 (12), Janos/AS; 17 (14), satou y1/AS; 18 (1), Matthew Mcclure/DR; 18 (3), Micha Klootwijk/DR; 18 (5), Jiri Vaclavek/DR; 18 (CTR), Mandacrab/DR; 18 (7), Carlos/AS; 18 (8), Chris & Monique Fallows/NPL; 18 (9), Matthew R McClure/SS; 19 (14), LuismiCSS/Getty Images; 19 (15), MS Creative Photography - Maarten Jozef Billen/ASP; 19 (16), Fata Morgana by Andrew Marriott/SS; 19 (17), Mark Kostich/AS; 19 (18), BW Folsom/SS; 19 (20), scubagreg123/AS; 19 (21), macbrianmun/SS; 19 (22), Doug Perrine/ASP; 20-21, Ralph Pace/Minden Pictures; 20 (1), Michael Rosskothen/AS; 20 (3), Mark Carwardine/NPL; 20 (5), vitstudio/SS; 20 (7), luchschenF/AS; 21 (9), Sergey Uryadnikov/DR; 21 (13), Doug Perrine/NPL; 21 (15), Ruth Black/AS; 22-23, Ralph Pace/Minden Pictures; 22 (1), Vitaly Krivosheev/AS; 22 (3), Anion/AS; 22 (5), prochym/AS; 23 (8), Wildlife GmbH/ASP; 23 (10), Doug Perrine/NPL; 23 (12), Alex Mustard/NPL; 23 (14), crisod/AS; 24 (1), Pvb969924/DR; 24 (2), zea_lenanet/AS; 24 (3), Michael Wood/DR; 24 (6), Luis Miguel Estévez/DR; 24 (7), Alex Mustard/NPL; 24 (9), Kelvin Aitken/VWPics/ASP; 24 (11), R. Gino Santa Maria/AS; 24 (13), Andrey Nekrasov/ASP; 25 (14), Pascal Kobeh/NPL; 25 (15), Andy Murch/NPL; 25 (18), aquapix/AS; 25 (19), Bill Curtsinger/National Geographic Image Collection; 25 (20), Alex Mustard/NPL; 25 (21), Insomniaticmuse/AS; 25 (23), LuisMiguel/AS; 25 (24), Pvb969924/DR; 26-27, crisod/AS; 26 (1), Four Oaks/SS; 26 (3), Izanbar/DR; 26 (5), Tom Versteege/DR; 26 (7), Tatiana Nurieva/AS; 27 (9), whitcomberd/AS; 27 (11), crisod/AS; 27 (13), Leith Holtzman/SS; 27 (15), wildestanimal/SS; 28-29, aquapix/AS; 30 (1), Andy Murch/Image Quest Marine; 30 (6), Jeff Milisen Blue Planet Archive; 30 (8), Doug Perrine/Blue Planet Archive; 30 (9), Jordi Chias/NPL; 30 (10 & 11), Kelvin Aitken/VWPics/ASP; 31 (13), JMallefet/FNRS/UCLouvain - Belgium; 31 (14), David Shale/NPL; 31 (15), Paulo de Oliveira/Biosphoto/Minden Pictures; 31 (17), Greg Amptman/DR; 31 (18), Roberto Nistri/ASP; 31 (19), Mariana Franco/DR; 31 (20), pixelrobot/AS; 31 (23), Michael Pitts/NPL; 32 (1), Norbert Wu/Minden Pictures; 32 (4), Jeff Rotman/NPL; 32 (6), Cphoto/DR; 32 (8), Michael Ansell/DR; 32-33, Alex Mustard/NPL 33 (10), Éric Isselée/AS; 33 (12), Jeff Rotman/NPL; 33 (14), Aozora/AS; 34 (1), Teguh Tirtaputra/DR; 34 (3), Sue Daly/NPL; 34 (5), Vincent Pommeyrol/DR; 34 (7), Petr Zamecnik/DR; 34 (8), LichtmaschineCGI/AS; 34 (9), Mark Strickland/Blue Planet Archive; 34 (12), Alexius Sutandio/SS; 35 (14), VisionDive/AS; 35 (15), jgolby/AS; 35 (17), Vladimir Wrangel/AS; 35 (18), Doug Perrine/Blue Planet Archive; 35 (19), Solvin Zankl/NPL; 35 (20), Norbert Wu/Minden Pictures; 35 (23), Juergen Freund/NPL; 36-37, wildestanimal/SS; 36 (1), wildestanimal/SS; 36 (3), crisod/AS; 36 (5), vkilikov/AS; 36 (7), Clara/AS; 37 (9), Vasily Smirnov/AS; 37 (11), Uryadnikov Sergey/AS; 37 (15), slowmotiongli/AS; 38 (1), bradlifestyle/SS; 38 (3), Alex Mustard/NPL; 38 (4), Greg Amptman/DR; 38 (6), ead72/AS; 38 (7), Andamanse/DR; 38 (8), wildestanimal/AS; 38 (11), IrinaK/SS; 38 (12), Vladimir Wrangel/AS; 39 (14), Yann Hubert/DR; 39 (16), Mark Strickland/Blue Planet Archive; 39 (17), Yann hubert/SS; 39 (19), Todd Winner/Stocktrek Images/Getty Images; 39 (21), OutdoorWorks/SS; 39 (22), James Dvorak/DR; 39 (24), Rodrigo Friscione/Getty Images; 40-41, Alex Mustard/NPL; 40 (1), Joern/AS; 40 (3), Maya_parf/AS; 40 (5), Richard Griffin/AS; 41 (8), Jag_cz/AS; 41 (10), Nick Everett/DR; 41 (14), Andy Murch/Blue Planet Archive; 42-43, Erik Kruthoff/DR; 42 (10), Tamara Bauer/DR; 42 (18), nbriam/AS; 42 (24), Thomas Lozinski/DR; 42 (28), Leonello Calvetti/DR; 42 (32), Michael Valos/DR; 43 (42), Antpun/DR; 44 (1 & 7), Alex Mustard/2020VISION/NPL; 44 (5), Mark Groves/Nature Photographers Ltd/ASP; 44 (8 & 11), Dan Burton/NPL; 45 (13), Chris Gomersall/NPL; 45 (15), Mike Clark/ASP; 45 (20), Vnikitenko/DR; 45 (21), Dbjohnston/DR; 45 (22), The Natural History Museum/ASP; 45 (24), prochym/AS; 46-47, Franco Banfi/NPL; 48 (1), Jeff Moore/DR; 48 (2), Jamiegodson/DR; 48 (3), Alex Mustard/NPL; 48 (7), Tony Wu/NPL; 48 (8), Dirk van der Heide/SS; 48 (9), Wafuefotodesign/DR; 48 (12), Ethan Daniels/DR; 49 (14 & 15), Alex Mustard/NPL; 49 (16), Joanne Weston/DR; 49 (18), Richard Carey/DR; 49 (19), Irko Van Der Heide/DR; 49 (23), Shane Gross/NPL; 49 (24), Insos Kampung/DR; 50-51, Martin Prochazkacz/SS; 50 (2), wildestanimal/SS; 50 (4), Gerard Soury/Getty Images; 50 (6), b.neeser/AS; 50 (8), Wrangel/DR; 51 (12), FtLaud/SS; 51 (10), Andy Murch/Blue Planet Archive; 51 (14), ilbusca/Getty Images; 52-53, Erica Niemi/ASP; 52 (2), Rocky W. Widner/NHL/Getty Images; 52 (4), Popova Olga/AS; 52 (6), Jakekohlberg/DR; 53 (10), Alexander Jung/SS; 53 (12), Anton_Ivanov/SS; 53 (14), Sony Herdiana/SS; 54 (1), Carol Buchanan/DR; 54 (4), Uli Jooss/culture-images GmbH/ASP; 54 (5), Brian Cahn/ZUMA Wire/Alamy Live News; 54 (7), Albert Lleal/Minden Pictures; 54 (9), Grace Chiu/UPI/ASP; 54 (12), Caters News/Zuma Press; 55 (13), U.S. Navy, Official Photograph; 55 (14), Andrey Suslov/SS; 55 (17), Lia Caldas/SS; 55 (19), Oleg Doroshin/DR; 55 (22), Lane Erickson/AS; 55 (23 & 24), SeaChange Technology/Getty Images; 56-57, crisod/AS; 58-59, Andrea Izzotti/AS; 58 (1), Michael Bogner/DR; 58 (3), Michael Herman/DR; 58 (5), Andrea Izzotti/AS; 59 (UP), Patryk Kosmider/DR; 59 (9), Willyam Bradberry/SS; 59 (11), Mbolina/DR; 59 (13), Andrea Izzotti/AS; 60 (1), shanemyersphoto/AS; 60 (4 & 5), Richard Robinson/NPL; 60 (6), frantisek hojdysz/AS; 60 (7), Toby Parsons/DR; 60 (8), Pascal Kobeh/NPL; 60 (9), Doug Perrine/NPL; 60 (12), Ronald C. Modra/Getty Images; 61 (13), Chris & Monique Fallows/NPL; 61 (16), Doug Perrine/Blue Planet Archive; 61 (17), Doug Perrine/NPL; 61 (19), Uryadnikov Sergey/AS; 61 (22), Andamanse/DR; 61 (24), bearacreative/AS; 62-63, Suzanne Long/ASP; 62 (1), ilbusca/Getty Images; 62 (3), Universal History Archive/Universal Images Group via Getty Images; 62 (7), Kelvin Aitken/VWPics/ASP; 63 (9), Gerald Corsi/Getty Images; 63 (11), Yu Haiyang/DR; 63 (15), North Wind Picture Archives/ASP; 64-65, Mark Carwardine/NPL; 64 (1), Franco Tempesta; 64 (3), sam/AS; 64 (7), Sinclair Stammers/Science Source; 65 (9), Millard H. Sharp/Science Source; 65 (11), Jim Roberts/DR; 65 (15), Franco Tempesta; 66-67, Kelpfish/DR; 68-69, David Scharf/Science Source; 68 (1), Fiona Ayerst/DR; 68 (3), David Fleetham/ASP; 68 (5), Choksawatdikorn/SS; 68 (7), George W. Benz/Blue Planet Archive; 69 (9), Solvin Zankl/NPL; 69 (11), Gary Bell/Oceanwide/Minden Pictures; 69 (13), Ayah Raushan/SS; 70 (1), Anatoliy Tesouro/SS; 70 (5), Rob Carr/Getty Images; 70 (6), Willsie/Getty Images; 70 (8), World History Archive/ASP; 70 (9), Universal Pictures/Photofest; 70 (10), ArliftAtoz2205/SS; 70 (12), carbouval/AS; 71 (13), Pixar Animation Studios/Walt Disney Pictures film/ASP; 71 (15), Alison Wright/ASP; 71 (16), DreamWorks/courtesy Everett Collection; 71 (18), Carmen K. Sisson/Cloudybright/ASP; 71 (20), ©Warner Brothers/courtesy Everett Collection; 71 (23), Evgeny Dubasov/DR; 71 (24), Elnur/DR; 72-73, Sue Daly/NPL; 72 (1), Susana_Martins/SS; 72 (3), Andy Murch/Blue Planet Archive; 72 (5), Greg Amptman/DR; 73 (UP), Good luck images/SS; 73 (9), Jeff Rotman/NPL; 73 (13), Melissaf84/DR; 73 (15), Kelvin Aitken/VWPics/ASP; 74 (1), Ralph Pace/Minden Pictures; 74 (3), JMallefet/FNRS/UCLouvain - Belgium; 74 (4), Doug Perrine/Blue Planet Archive; 74 (5), Divedog/DR; 74 (7), Mark Conlin/Blue Planet Archive; 74 (8), Makoto Hirose/e-Photo/Blue Planet Archive; 74 (9), Kelvin Aitken/VWPics/AS; 74 (10), dottedyeti/AS; 75 (13), Magnus Lundgren/NPL; 75 (14), Jeremy Stafford-Deitsch/Blue Planet Archive; 75 (16), Doug Perrine/NPL; 75 (CTR RT), Igor Gromoff/AS; 75 (19), Doug Perrine/NPL; 75 (21), Jeff Rotman/NPL; 75 (22), ArteSub/ASP; 75 (23), Fiona Ayerst/DR; 75 (24), Wildlife GmbH/ASP; 76-77, Sue Flood/ASP; 76 (1), Dominique Charriau/WireImage/Getty Images; 76 (3), Valerie Macon/Getty Images; 76 (5), kudryavtsev dmitriy/SS; 76 (7), Michael Cole/Corbis via Getty Images; 77 (11), Victor Virgile/Gamma-Rapho via/Getty Images; 77 (13), Paul Brown/ASP; 77 (15), Kent Johnson/AS; 78-79, Mark Strickland/Blue Planet Archive; 80-81, Pete Oxford/Minden Pictures; 80 (3), David Doubilet/National Geographic Image Collection; 80 (5), oliver leedham/ASP; 80 (7), MARKA/AS; 81 (12), ullstein bild/ullstein bild via Getty Images; 81 (14), Brian J. Skerry/National Geographic Image Collection; 81 (15), Wirestock/DR; 82-83, Pascal Kobeh/NPL; 82 (3), Bruce Rasner/Rotman/NPL; 82 (5), Sergio Hanquet/NPL; 83 (UP), Brocreative/AS; 83 (11), Andy Murch/Blue Planet Archive; 83 (14), Pascal Kobeh/NPL; 84-85, scubagreg123/AS; 85 (22), Dennis Sabo/DR; 85 (42), Natthapon Ngamnithiporn/DR; 86-87, Brendon Thorne/Getty Images; 86 (1), Karel Bartik/SS; 86 (5), aerial-drone/AS; 86 (7), Ocean Conservancy; 87 (9), Doug Perrine/NPL; 87 (11), Ethan Daniels/SS; 87 (15), Richard Milnes/ASP; 88, Dorling Kindersley ltd/ASP; 89 (UP LE), Leopoldo Palomba/DR; 89 (CTR RT), pbnew/AS; 89 (LO), Ian Coleman/NPL; 90 (UP LE), Dan Bagur/SS; 90 (LO RT), Mark Conlin/VWPics/ASP; 90 (UP RT), tonaquatic/AS; 91 (UP), Picture Partners/AS; 91 (CTR RT), LuisMiguel/AS; 91 (LO), Ian Scott/DR; 91 (CTR LE), Nerthuz/DR; 92 (UP LE), Valerii Evlakhov/AS; 92 (UP RT), wildestanimal/SS; 92 (CTR RT), Juvencio Fuentes Nolasco/SS; 92 (LO LE), Dusseauphoto/AS; 92 (LO LE), Travel_Master/AS; 92 (CTR LE), Fiona Ayerst/SS; 93 (chimaeriformes), Greg Amptman/DR; 93 (rajiformes), Picture Partners/AS; 93 (heterodontiformes), Travel_Master/AS; 93 (orectolobiformes), Ian Scott/DR; 93 (lamniformes), wildestanimal/SS; 93 (carcharhiniformes), Dusseauphoto/AS; 93 (hexanchiformes), Fiona Ayerst/SS; 93 (pristiophoriformes), Juvencio Fuentes Nolasco/SS; 93 (squaliformes), dottedyeti/AS; 93 (squatiniformes), Luis Miguel Estevez/AS; 95, cherylvb/AS

Since 1888, the National Geographic Society has funded more than 14,000 research, conservation, education, and storytelling projects around the world. National Geographic Partners distributes a portion of the funds it receives from your purchase to National Geographic Society to support programs including the conservation of animals and their habitats. To learn more, visit natgeo.com/info.

For more information, visit nationalgeographic.com, call 1-877-873-6846, or write to the following address:

National Geographic Partners, LLC
1145 17th Street NW
Washington, DC 20036-4688 U.S.A.

For librarians and teachers: nationalgeographic.com/books/librarians-and-educators

More for kids from National Geographic: natgeokids.com

National Geographic Kids magazine inspires children to explore their world with fun yet educational articles on animals, science, nature, and more. Using fresh storytelling and amazing photography, *Nat Geo Kids* shows kids ages 6 to 14 the fascinating truth about the world—and why they should care. natgeo.com/subscribe

For rights or permissions inquiries, please contact National Geographic Books Subsidiary Rights: bookrights@natgeo.com

Designed by Brett Challos

Hardcover ISBN: 978-1-4263-7174-5
Reinforced library binding ISBN: 978-1-4263-7175-2

Printed in China
23/LPC/1